SPEAK LIKE A CEO

SECRETS FOR COMMANDING ATTENTION AND GETTING RESULTS

SUZANNE BATES

Mc
Graw
Hill
Education

New York   Chicago   San Francisco   Athens   London   Madrid
Mexico City   Milan   New Delhi   Singapore   Sydney   Toronto

1 2 3 4 5 6 7 8 9   QFR   22 21 20 19 18 17

ISBN   978-1-260-11748-6
MHID   1-260-11748-0

e-ISBN   978-0-07-146617-2
e-MHID   0-07-146617-7

McGraw-Hill Education books are available at special quantity discounts to use as premiums and sales promotions or for use in corporate training programs. To contact a representative, please visit the Contact Us pages at www.mhprofessional.com.

Praise for *Speak like a CEO*

"Speak like a CEO *is practical, helpful, insightful, and comforting. Suzanne Bates helps leaders (even the most podium-shy) learn how to find their natural and authentic voice. And she does this with an informed understanding of the real everyday work of leaders."*

—ROSABETH MOSS KANTER, Author of the National Bestseller *Confidence: How Winning Streaks and Losing Streaks Begin and End*

"*Suzanne Bates's book provides a wealth of usable information in an easy-to-use format that will prove useful and effective for leaders in all sectors: public, private, or not-for-profit. At the end of the day, whether you are the CEO of a company or a government leader, the efficacy of your leadership is dependent on not only the quality of your ideas but your ability to effectively communicate them. Execution depends on energizing and engaging key groups of influencers, and communication that engenders support and enthusiasm is a necessary skill."*

—JANE SWIFT, Former Governor of Massachusetts

"*It is neither the smartest nor the hardest working CEO who succeeds in business. It is the one who best communicates his or her firm's vision to customers, vendors, and employees.* Speak like a CEO *shows you how."*

—TOM STEMBERG, CEO of Staples

"*In* Speak like a CEO, *Suzanne Bates points out that the skill set needed to rise within an organization does not usually include the single skill most needed as one rises closer to the top: the ability to communicate. In a book that manages to encourage personalization of style even as it prescribes the steps that need to be taken to become a more effective speaker and presenter, Bates succeeds by showing rather than telling. In doing so, it becomes clear that* Speak like a CEO *is for any of us who wish to stand up in front of an audience with greater confidence, preparedness, and ability to connect. Clearly it is not just a book for CEOs.*"

—RUSSELL T. ABBOTT, Principal, Treflie Capital Management

"*Suzanne has written a book based on solid research and nailed key concepts regarding communication and leadership in a clear, concise, and entertaining way.*"

—ANNE HAWLEY STEVENS, Founder and Managing Partner, ClearRock, Inc.

"*A practical how-to guide. Reading this book may not make you a CEO, but it should make you sound like one.*"

—CHARLES STEIN, Business Columnist, *Boston Globe*

"*Executive presence, leadership, and style—three great attributes that can easily be achieved by reading this book.*"

—MARY LOU ANDRE, Author, *Ready to Wear: An Expert's Guide to Choosing and Using Your Wardrobe*

"*I was amazed at how accurately this book captures the challenges that CEOs face everyday.* Speak like a CEO *is insightful, honest, and instructive. It is a must read for people who want to be taken seriously as a public speaker.*"

—PAMELA J. MONTPELIER, President and CEO, Strata Bank

To Drew and Meghan

Contents

PART 1

The Secrets: What CEOs and Leaders Know

PART 2

The Situations: A Survival Guide for the Events Where You Must Speak and Be Great

PART 3

The Strategies: Become a Great Speaker by Making a Plan and Working It

Preface to the Paperback Edition

WHEN MCGRAW-HILL TOLD ME that they were publishing a paperback edition of *Speak like a CEO*, I was delighted. Just about every week I hear from people who keep a dog-eared copy on their shelves, routinely lend copies to colleagues, and recommend it to their friends and employees. *Speak like a CEO* has been published in many languages and has maintained a place on bestseller lists. Many people have told me that they consider it a must-read for leaders and aspiring leaders, and for that I am humbled and grateful.

When my editor asked me to write a new preface, I wasn't sure at first how to proceed. It has been several years, and a few subsequent books, since I have had the chance to sit down and read it. Several questions and concerns crossed my mind. Would the advice still prove relevant? Was it still fresh, in a world that is more global and better connected by technology?

The digital age has transformed the way we live, work, and communicate. We now have many choices. We can hold a virtual, face-to-face meeting from anywhere on the planet. We can lead dispersed teams in distant business locations. Our employees and customers are everywhere, and expect to reach us 24/7. Want proof? Try posting an out of office message claiming that you have limited access to e-mail. No one will believe it. Everyone knows that we are all always connected.

The communication evolution has been felt most acutely in the proliferation of social media and social platforms. Social networks have both empowered us and disrupted us. Participating in social media is no longer a choice. Instead, it has become a must-have tool to build your business or platform. If you work at a business, you need to get into the conversation. I remember a time when executive clients used to ask me *whether* they should tweet, blog, or do podcasts. Today they ask *how*. They know if they don't do it, their competitors will be ahead of the game.

If you take advantage of the proliferation of communication technology, the door is open to building a formidable presence. Writing and speaking with new technology enables you to connect with customers, employees, investors, analysts, and the media. If you want to, you can become a thought leader through your own efforts. You don't have to wait for the media to find you because you can create your own channels. People can find you in many places—on LinkedIn, Facebook, and a proliferating number of other social networks.

It's all exciting but, as we all know, this new world is loaded with land mines. You have a reputation to protect. That is harder today. News, business, and entertainment outlets demand content. This means they value speed over accuracy. The competition has also blurred the lines between journalism and advocacy, as commentary abounds. With mobile technology in everyone's hands, there is no privacy. Citizen journalists can capture pictures and sound and post it to the world.

Reflecting on these changes, I opened *Speak like a CEO*, and surprised even myself. What I discovered was that it is relevant—perhaps more than ever. For all that has changed, what has not changed is that as leaders, we must communicate effectively with our important audiences. This digital, connected world demands that we master these skills. We can choose *how to do it*, but we do not have a choice *whether* or not to do it well.

I hope that as you look to the chapters of the book you'll find advice you can use right away to communicate—in any media form—with impact and influence. *Speak like a CEO* was always meant to be a practice guide to help leaders because some things never change. We still need to understand our audience, be able to organize a powerful message, and tell a story. These are not natural born skills. The good news is that they are skills anyone can learn.

Whether you were born in the digital age, or you remember a black and white television in your living room and 8-track tapes in your car, you know that change is inevitable. Technology will keep advancing. We will always be challenged to learn something new. Some futurists believe that we will be communicating full, rich thoughts to each other through brain-to-brain telepathy. My dog already knows how to do that. But then, dogs have always been more evolved than humans.

Technology advances. The principles of good communication remain constant. I hope this will be a timeless guide to delivering a message that is powerful and memorable. Leadership demands that we do this. Leadership is not about title, position, or authority. It's about influence. What this book is, and has always been about, is the art and science of communicating to engage people's hearts and minds.

Preface to the Hardcover Edition

BEING THE TOP PERSON in any organization is a great accomplishment, but it's tough. Today, people expect more than ever of their leaders. Whether you are CEO, president, managing partner, executive director, owner, publisher, editor, king, or commander in chief, people expect more. You work hard and make the most of luck to reach the top. Then you work harder to keep the job.

If you aspire to the top job, you not only have to know your *business*—you have to know how to communicate with everyone else inside and outside the business. The higher you go, and the more visible you are, the more communication counts. You're competing in a global world with *instant* communication. There is no forgiveness for the leader who can't keep up.

My company is in the business of improving executive performance with better communications. I call it "Tuning the Voice of Leadership." This book shares techniques and skills that have helped many executives and professionals do just that.

Once you arrive in the top jobs, you're expected to know what to do. Often we find our clients are surprised. Their early roles have not prepared them for the speaking roles. As you move up the ladder, you don't necessarily get opportunities to do what you need to when you're the boss. You've been promoted for your business skill; now you have to develop a whole new set of competencies.

Why do you need to speak well if you're a leader or if you aspire to be? It's simple: the smartest people aren't necessarily the ones who rise to the top. It's the ones who can communicate well. If you don't learn to speak like a leader, you are in danger of being passed over for your dream job. This book will show you how to develop a personalized plan for mastering the skills you need.

Whether you are the boss or you want to be, this book addresses some of the missing links. You will learn the principles for communicating *like a leader*—the things they don't tell you in college or even on your way up.

Why I Wrote This Book

When I began coaching executives after twenty years in television news, I was struck by how little formal training leaders had in public speaking. Some had never attended any formal classes or worked with a coach. Some had been through a day or two of group training. Yet, they were expected to speak to large groups, deliver major keynotes, appear at important industry conferences, lead board meetings, talk to news reporters, and manage other high-pressure situations. I realized that there was a need for a book that provides a *sophisticated* approach to speaking well and projecting authentic leadership.

In this book, you will discover some of the secrets that I have discovered during my years in the media and then as an executive coach. The goal of this book is to share ideas that can help you develop a credible, authoritative leadership presence. The ideas and programs should shorten the learning curve and eliminate the pain of trial and error. If you incorporate these ideas and work the programs, it will transform you from a so-so speaker or presenter to a good one.

Who Should Read This Book?

Even if you have experience making presentations; running meetings; talking to reporters; or participating in panels, conferences, and seminars, you will learn valuable lessons on how to make it in the big leagues of business here. Even professionals in the field—television and radio hosts, news anchors, and people who make a living at speaking—are lifelong learners when it comes to communication skill. Top businesspeople must invest time every year in improving their communication skills if they want to have an impact as thought leaders in their industries.

What You Will Learn

The advice in this book goes beyond what you might find in a one-size-fits-all book on public speaking. This is not a standard book on presentation skills—it is a book that emphasizes the communication skills *leaders* must have to succeed. When you finish this book, you will be able to create a personalized plan for self-development and be well on your way to becoming an authentic and credible speaker in front of crowds and cameras.

Through exercises and self-assessments, you'll learn to recognize and develop your own style. You'll find nuts-and-bolts advice on how to improve speeches, presentations, and media interviews in both content and style. Tips and techniques will help you develop your own authentic, natural style and provide you with last-minute help to reduce the preperformance jitters. There's also advice on how to speak in sound bites for TV, radio, or print. You'll find out how to handle tough questions from a pack of reporters, ways to warm up an audience and keep people engaged—plus much more.

Beyond the mechanics of speaking and appearing like a leader, you'll learn how to win the trust of others so that they become willing to listen to your ideas, understand your vision, and execute your strategies. The various chapters feature numerous examples of leaders who speak well and explanations of how they do it so you can adapt it to your own authentic speaking style.

How to Get the Most out of This Book:
You Decide the Best Plan for You

The book includes practical advice, inspiration, and a blueprint for developing your own authentic speaking style. There are several ways to use the book—it's up to you.

- You can read the text all the way through to get an overview of how to speak like a CEO or an authentic leader.

- You can work on one aspect of communication skills over the coming months, especially if the subject is new to you. You may, for example, feel confident giving speeches but not as comfortable handling the press. Whatever you believe is a priority, turn directly to that chapter and begin.

- After you have read the book, you can refer to the end of each of the "situation" chapters in Part 2 for tips to help you prepare for speeches, presentations, meetings, and media interviews. Look for the "Summary" section, with entries listed by the categories "Last-minute tip," "If you have more time," and "Plan for ongoing improvement."

- Finally, you can use this book as a complete coaching guide: read it through, and work the strategies and recommended plans in Part 3 to create your own coaching plan. You may also want to hire a coach; Part 3 includes advice on what to do and how to guarantee your success.

Many people believe that speaking is a "nice-to-have" or "soft" skill that should have little impact on their ability to rise to the top. But on the balance sheet of business, not knowing how to speak is a liability. No one who is serious about leading an organization would ignore a liability. Those who are serious would take note and start doing the things that build the asset side of the balance sheet.

In my experience, leaders really want and need information about how to speak well. While there are many books and courses on public speaking, most of them tend to focus on just the basics of presentation skills. There is absolutely nothing wrong with these books—read them! But if you believe you are beyond the basics, and you want to join the ranks of great leaders who speak well, read on. What you want is not only possible, but it is likely, if you apply what you learn here.

Acknowledgments

MANY FRIENDS AND COLLEAGUES have made this book possible. I am deeply grateful for the advice, encouragement, and support of Jenna Furdon, Ken Lizotte, Karen Hansen, Donya Dickerson, Lara Murphy, Mary Glenn, Tara Frier, Margrette Mondillo, Annie Stevens, Chris Storr, Mary Lou Andre, Marcia Abbott, Paula Lyons, Ann Conway, Jim Norman, Janet Patterson, Eleanor Uddo, Vickie Sullivan, Marcia Reynolds, Karen Friedman, Cheryl Richardson, Aleta Koman, Ginger Applegarth, Ginny Rehberg, Kasey Kaufman, Frank Ciota, Lisa Zankman, Margery Myers, Bob Lobel, Vicki Donlan, Kathy Venne, Gayle Sierens, and Mom and Dad.

CEOs and leaders have generously contributed their time and wisdom. I am indebted to Charlie Baker, President and CEO, Harvard Pilgrim Health Care; Judy George, founder and CEO, Domain Home Furnishings; Tom Goemaat, President and CEO, Shawmut Design and Construction; John Hamill, Chairman and CEO, Sovereign Bank of New England; Paul Levy, CEO, Beth Israel Deaconess Medical Center (Harvard); Larry Lucchino, CEO, Boston Red Sox; Phil Lussier, President, Institutional Division, Citistreet; Chris Moore, CEO, Live Planet; Lori Morrissette, VP Human Resources, Citistreet; Ann Murphy, VP, O'Neill Associates; Tom O'Neill, President and CEO, O'Neill Associates; Peter Rollins, Chief Executives Club, Boston College; Dan Wolf, founder, President, and CEO, Cape Air and Nantucket Airlines; and Arnold Zetcher, President and CEO, Talbots.

Introduction

IF YOU'VE EVER HAD a great boss, chances are that boss knew how to communicate well. Leaders who communicate well have a big advantage over those who come to the job with just experience and technical skill. Experience and technical skill are assumed in those who rise to the top. Leaders who communicate well succeed because they can also *articulate* vision, *share* wisdom, and *motivate* others to action.

Leaders have different styles of communicating. There is no one right way. There is no cookie-cutter approach to communicating as a leader. The most successful leaders blend an authentic, unique style with the best techniques and become extremely effective.

Leaders do not succeed when they copy, imitate, or adopt someone else's style. Leaders succeed when they do it their way. People see them as genuine leaders when they are *genuine*. Authenticity inspires trust. Trust creates willingness. Willingness creates successful organizations.

A unique, authentic style is critical to a leader's success. You have to communicate in your unique way. Yes, you have to know the rules of the road to drive the car, or you won't get where you are going. But once you know the rules, you must drive your own car, your way. You must develop your own, authentic voice of leadership. *Speak like a CEO* will help you learn the rules of the road—the secrets of communicating well—*and* find your unique voice. You will discover how to be you and be a leader.

Speak like a CEO isn't going to tell you who to be. You have to figure out who you are. You have to learn the rules of the road *and* find your own authentic voice of leadership if you want to speak like a CEO.

Finding your unique voice is tremendously powerful. It helps you transcend your title, to reach a position of true leadership. Your authentic voice is why you were hired for your job and how you will get people to listen so you can succeed. You, and only you, have been brought to this organization at this time because of your way of doing things. You owe it to yourself and your organization to allow that authentic voice to be heard.

It is a lot easier to be you than to pretend to be someone you are not. A lot of people put on power suits and look the part. There's nothing wrong with a great suit, but an ordinary leader in a great suit is still an ordinary leader—not a person who inspires trust. The real you must emerge and lead in order for your enterprise to succeed.

If you are a leader, or want to be, you owe it to yourself and your organization to communicate well, in your unique authentic style. You cannot be mediocre. You cannot be ordinary or average. A mediocre or average communicator risks being marginalized or deemed irrelevant. A marginalized or irrelevant leader is dangerous to an organization. You have to communicate well, your way, so people believe in you. People must believe in you to be willing to follow.

This is a different kind of book on speaking—it is for CEOs and people who want to be leaders and speak with an authentic voice. You will learn far more than the basics of presentation style or media interviews or leading meetings; you will learn what you need to do to find that unique leadership voice. Whether you are the CEO or *want* to be the CEO someday, you have an opportunity right now, today, to develop and grow one of your greatest assets—the authentic voice of leadership.

PART 1

The Secrets

What CEOs and Leaders Know

What It Means to Speak like a CEO (the Ones You Really Admire)

"Every time you have to speak,
you are auditioning for leadership."

—JAMES HUMES, American Lawyer, Speaker, and Author

The CEO's Role

The chief executive officer is the highest authority in the day-to-day management of a corporation. This person usually has the ultimate executive power within an organization or company. The CEO usually reports to, and is a member of, the company's board of directors. The CEO may also be the chairperson of the board in small companies, although the two roles are separated in larger organizations. Either way, it's a big job.

A CEO is responsible to every employee, every member of the board, and every customer or client, as well as the community and sometimes the industry. How can any CEO succeed without communicating well? It's impossible.

The title of this chapter includes the parenthetical "the ones you really admire" because not *all* CEOs speak well. Some speak poorly. Some hardly communicate. For those CEOs, there are consequences.

Those who speak poorly are marginalized. Those who rarely communicate alarm people when they *do*. Business is about nothing but communication. One top CEO describes why rarely communicating is ineffective: "It's like blood through an artery: if you have never communicated and then suddenly do—*whatever* you say will be overwhelmed by the mere fact that you have just communicated."

Leading is all about communicating. The leader's job is generally not to *do*; it is to communicate what is to be done. People must see, hear, feel, and believe in the vision. They must see, hear, and believe in *you*. You are the message, and the message is you.

Whenever people are asked about the most important skill of a leader, communication is always at the top of the list. Even when CEOs were asked (in a 2002 survey by *Chief Executive* magazine and Hill & Knowlton) to state the most significant thing they could do (other than increase financial performance) to improve the company's reputation, the top response was "communicating to customers." Number two was "communicating to employees."

Look at the busy schedule of a CEO on an average day, and you'll see just how important communication is. Mike Eskew, chairman and CEO of UPS, says the itinerary of a typical business trip looks much like this:

- Speak informally to drivers in the morning
- Meet with various management people for focus groups and town hall assemblies
- Attend recognition events
- Sit down with the customers and discuss their issues and concerns
- Sit down with the press
- Meet with stakeholders—whether it's business partners or community leaders

There is nothing on CEO Mike Eskew's busy schedule from morning to night but talking and listening. That's the job requirement. That's what CEOs do.

Why You Must Speak Well: The Spotlight Is Always on You

The CEO of a firm with four hundred employees and $430 million in revenue confided to me, "It would be nice to be invisible once in a while." Unfortunately, you cannot wish the spotlight away. When you're the CEO, you are in it 24-7. Somebody is always watching.

"It's not just public speaking," the CEO explained. "It is body language, every minute of every day. If I walk around moping, they don't think something is wrong with *me*; they think something is wrong with the *company*." He continued, "I have learned not to mope. It doesn't mean you're not real with people. You have to be real. But you have to remember it's not just about you."

Nationwide Survey: Leaders and Communication

Bates Communications wanted to understand more about the authentic leader, so, in 2004, we conducted a study on how bosses communicate. The online survey of 293 professionals revealed that people were disappointed. Most participants said their bosses didn't communicate well, even though they indicated that communication is one of the most important skills a boss can have.

We asked participants to rate their bosses on ten dimensions of leadership and to discuss their communication styles. We also asked about authenticity and leadership. We gave them an opportunity to answer both multiple-choice and open-ended questions.

The results show how important communication is in the workplace. Only 29 percent of participants working in professional services firms, corporations, and private companies said there were enough articulate voices of leadership in their organizations. Yet, more than 90 percent said communication is a *critical* dimension of leadership. There is a disconnect between the kind of leadership that organizations have and what they need. The bottom line for bosses: it's time to learn to communicate more effectively.

How important is it for the leader of your organization to communicate effectively?

91.5%   Very important—it's a critical dimension of leadership

7.8%   Somewhat important—it contributes to our success

.7%   Not very important—other skills are much more critical

While most people said they respect their leaders, they also said they would like them to communicate better. More than one-third said they would be surprised, or even shocked, if the head of their company were to speak to the organization and inspire others to follow.

How surprised would you be if the head of your company were to speak to the organization, clearly articulating a new direction and inspiring everyone to follow?

65.5%   Not surprised—this person is an authentic voice of leadership

26.3%   Somewhat surprised—we rarely see that ability to articulate or inspire

8.2%   Shocked—this leader just doesn't know how to do that

The assessment was even worse for managers and executives who are in the *pipeline* to leadership.

How would you characterize the voices of leadership in your organization?

29.0%   There are many articulate, inspiring leaders

49.8%   There are some, but we could use more

21.2%   There are few, if any, true voices of leadership here

---

Top leadership received better marks, but the findings showed a clear need for more and better voices of leadership throughout the ranks of most companies and organizations.

Since most people know more about their own bosses than the CEO, we asked respondents to rate their immediate superiors on a variety of communication dimensions. These bosses fared worse in the ratings on communication skills (listening, speaking skills, leading productive meetings) than on dimensions having to do with personal rapport (humor, candidness) or being the public face of an organization (articulating goals, representing the company). This indicates that bosses have the raw material, but learning communication techniques could only enhance their ability to lead.

Bosses scored lowest on the skills that leaders arguably need most: only 40 percent of the people surveyed said their bosses could lead productive meetings, 41 percent said their bosses were skilled at sharing critical information, and just 43 percent said the boss knew how to motivate and inspire others. This is not a resounding vote of confidence. In many other business areas, such as customer service, a 40 percent success rate would put you out of business.

The Cost of Poor Communication

What happens to bosses who don't learn to communicate well? Their employees do not trust what they say and seek information elsewhere.

Only about half of the people surveyed said that they learn what's going on with the boss by listening to what he or she says. The rest "watch" body language, listen to tone of voice, or go so far as to ask somebody else in the organization.

How do you generally tell what's going on with your boss?

52.2% By listening to what he or she says
32.8% By observing his or her face, body language, and tone of voice
15.0% By talking with other people about what they think

What makes an authentic leader? The survey asked two open-ended questions. Bates Communications categorized the respondents' answers into ten key dimensions of leadership. The number one quality that authentic leaders conveyed was honesty/integrity. Since these were open-ended responses, we treated them as qualitative data, but each of the dimensions was mentioned by dozens of respondents. Integrity in some form was mentioned by well over half.

Here is the leadership value system articulated by the survey's 293 respondents, in roughly descending order:

Honesty/Integrity. People who mentioned integrity referred to both business dealings and personal interactions. The words used to frame this concept were *honesty, integrity, ethics, fairness, candor, sincerity, trustworthiness,* and *truthfulness*—qualities that bosses must communicate through what they say and do.

Vision. Good leaders should have a vision for the organization, be able to articulate it, and inspire action. Vision was near the top of the list of leadership dimensions mentioned by respondents. It is not enough to be able to manage projects or people; authentic leadership entails the ability to visualize the future and effectively communicate that vision to others. Those who aspire to lead should take note. You can stay in middle management forever without this skill set. You will rise to the top if you can see the big picture and help others see it too.

Listening. This dimension includes several ways in which bosses should listen. They should be approachable and open to suggestions, open-minded, flexible, and willing to listen to everyone's ideas and feedback. Participants said seeking other points of view and actively listening to what others say are also critical.

Giving Feedback. What people most often mentioned in this category is the importance of giving credit where credit is due, including public praise for a job well done. Also high on the list was offering positive feedback when deserved and valuing employees' contributions. Feedback is not just a once-a-year process you build into your calendar. Regular, constructive feedback is essential to developing rapport, winning trust, and being seen as an authentic leader.

Emotional Intelligence. Emotional intelligence can be interpreted as the ability to communicate empathy and compassion, treat people well, and relate to them on a human level. Your demeanor counts: having a positive attitude and remaining calm under pressure send important signals through the organization. Emotional intelligence also means obvious passion for the work, a demonstrated commitment to the organization's success, and appreciation for those who make it happen. Authentic leaders use their emotional intelligence to connect and have genuine professional relationships.

Clarity. Clarity is a major theme here. People focus on your ability to articulate ideas and communicate clearly and convincingly with people at all levels. If the message is unclear, the team will not know how to do the things leaders ask. Confusion dilutes effort, and desired results are diminished. Without clarity, no one views a leader as authentic.

Knowledge and Intelligence. This topic received fewer mentions, probably because people presume an authentic leader has demonstrated de facto intelligence and mastery in the field. However, quite a few of the people surveyed mentioned that an authentic leader needs to be smart in every sense of the word and needs to have extensive knowledge of the substance of his or her field.

Managerial Skills. Participants mentioned the ability to delegate and allocate resources (monetary, physical, and human resources) for greatest effectiveness and efficiency. They also discussed ability to empower employees and trust them to get the job done, in other words, creating willingness in the organization.

Follow-Through. Authentic leaders practice what they preach. They walk the walk, and employees watch for this. Leaders follow through by spelling out goals. Leaders don't leave people hanging. Leaders are consistently concerned about how things come out, not just how they begin.

Humility. No one is perfect, especially leaders. People say authentic leaders have humility. They are willing to seek information. They ask for advice. They admit mistakes. They are willing to take appropriate risks. When mistakes occur, they graciously accept the consequences and take one for the team without pointing the finger of blame.

Survey Conclusions

The survey shows that leaders have to be able to communicate many qualities if they are to be seen as authentic and be given the power to lead. Title or position is far less important than projecting these qualities in what you say and do. People are longing for leaders with integrity, vision, and wisdom. They are longing for leaders who are authentic, real, and true to themselves and the organization. The survey is summarized in Appendix D.

Defining Authentic Leadership Style

What makes a leader authentic? Authenticity is something true. In a person, it's someone who *is* as he or she *appears* to be. This requires a degree of openness. You have to be willing to reveal something of yourself. One vice president admires her CEO because "he's willing to open up to people." The importance of this is simple, she said. "His being open makes people feel they can trust him."

Developing Your Unique Voice

A senior-level bank vice president was getting frequent requests to speak, but she often said no, because she was too busy. She hated to write speeches, resented the time investment, and never felt she delivered them well. She felt she was reciting lines from a marketing brochure. She never really felt that the words were coming from her. One day, she was invited to speak at a worldwide conference — an incredible opportunity — and she knew that a standard speech with the old "marketing" messages wasn't going to fly with this crowd.

She hired my company as her coach, and we went to work bringing her unique voice to the presentation. As we talked, she told me stories about people who had inspired her to succeed. She also told me story after story of successful women entrepreneurs who had received help from her bank, overcome the odds, and succeeded in business. Together we turned those reflections into powerful messages for her audience. The result was not only a good speech but also an experience of a lifetime. She soon began to receive invitations to speak at other prestigious events. Suddenly, she was in a highly visible position in her industry. Her authentic voice had emerged, and there was no turning back. She raised the visibility of her division, met people from all over the world, and enjoyed her work until she left to start her own consulting business. She was able to make that choice because of the visibility and recognition that public speaking provided her.

Speaking well opens doors. Speaking well gives you options. It creates opportunities. It takes you where you want to go. Through the proven techniques in this book, you'll learn how to use your communication skills to achieve your dreams, too.

The Myth of the Natural-Born Speaker

Mario Cuomo, the former governor of New York, who speaks with a unique, authentic voice, was terrified of speaking when he was growing up. As a child, he lived above a grocery store, where the family spoke only Italian at home. He never gave a speech in high school and lost himself in books instead. In college, he received an incomplete in a speech class because he didn't show up for the final exam. When he signed a contract with the Pittsburgh Pirates at the age of twenty-one, the scouting report said, "He's a very difficult fellow to get to know." The first speech Cuomo ever gave was in the Court of Appeals of the State of New York. He studied his subject until he knew it as well as humanly possible. He wrote and rewrote ideas to get ready. It was a success.

A lot of people assume great speakers talk off-the-cuff. They don't. As Cuomo puts it, "There's no comparison between the improvised speech and the one you've prepared." Great speakers *look* as if they can just get up and talk, because they are that good—they hardly use notes, and the words just flow.

There is no such thing as a natural-born speaker. That's a myth. The secret lies in learning the skills, just as you learn to tie your shoes or solve an algebra problem. You can't blame your gene pool if you're not a good speaker. But if you want to, you can learn to speak like a CEO. It's a talent you can develop.

What It Takes to Speak Well

Tom O'Neill is president and CEO of O'Neill Associates, a public relations and lobbying firm with thirty employees. A brilliant speaker and gifted storyteller, he became lieutenant governor of Massachusetts before launching his firm in 1982. You might think O'Neill would have inherited speaking skill from his father, former House Speaker Tip O'Neill.

But the younger O'Neill told me that as a young man, he was both a lazy and lousy speaker: further proof that public speaking is not an inheritable gene.

Freshman year in college, O'Neill's first assignment in communications was to prepare a five-minute speech on any topic. O'Neill showed up with nothing prepared, figuring he would wing it. Thirty seconds into the speech, the professor at the back of the class interrupted him and said, "Sit down, Mr. O'Neill."

The following week, the second assignment was to recite a poem from memory, and again O'Neill thought he could surely wing it. As he stood up to speak, the professor interrupted again. "Let me guess, Mr. O'Neill—'If,' by Rudyard Kipling." O'Neill stood dumbfounded. How had the professor known? "Sit down, Mr. O'Neill," said the professor. He had correctly guessed that O'Neill was about to recite a poem he had learned as a child.

O'Neill said he learned an important lesson from this experience. "I knew that if I was ever going to be a good public speaker, I had to know my subject, and I couldn't be predictable," he said. Cuomo learned the same lesson—he was never going to be a great speaker unless he worked at it. Good speaking skills aren't in your blood; they're in your *preparation*.

Assessing Your Skills

Since people are watching you all the time whether you like it or not, you might as well know what they think. If no one has ever told you how well you communicate, it's time to find out. It's far better to know what you need to do than to discover later that your lack of skills is holding you back. If you are a C or a D in the public speaking department, how can you be an A-plus as a CEO?

Great leaders don't say, "Speaking is not my forte." They see it as part of the job. Once you embrace it, it's easier. You learn it. You do it. You see tangible results.

By the way, the advice here isn't just for CEOs; it's for anyone who leads or wants to lead. It's for presidents, senior leaders, directors, managing partners, vice presidents, and people who want those jobs, too. The secrets here will help you discover your authentic voice of leadership and unique style. Every leader who wants to move up and stay there needs to develop an authentic leadership voice.

Doing this for yourself is important. But it's also important to your entire organization. Everyone who works for you counts on you to do the job at the highest level. Your associates are counting on you to communicate well and to be the voice and face of the organization.

Growing Your Assets

In business, you have to watch the balance sheet and continue to grow your assets. On your *personal* balance sheet, you also have assets to grow. Those are not your paycheck, job title, corporate revenue, or stock price; those items are the profits of your work. Your assets are your skills and talents. One of the most valuable of those is an authentic voice of leadership. Leaders who speak with an authentic voice—who can communicate well—have a distinct advantage in business.

Fortunately, you have lots of opportunities to grow this asset and develop an authentic voice of leadership, because every day, you have to communicate. You can't turn it on and off—or decide one day you will communicate, the next you won't. The job of a leader is to communicate. This is one asset you must develop to a high level, right away.

Most remarkable leaders will tell you they were average or even lousy speakers and writers when they started. You rarely meet CEOs who have always enjoyed getting up in front of a crowd. However, after gaining more experience, they have embraced public speaking. Mastery changes everything. Speaking is more fun when you do it well, in your own, unique voice.

Conclusion

So, rising to the top—becoming an authentic leader—is really about projecting the qualities that others look for in leaders, and doing it in your unique voice and style. You communicate these qualities, and you do it your way. You connect with people because you embody the qualities they want in a leader and they believe you are the real thing.

Speaking like a CEO is really all about projecting a set of qualities and doing it your way. So, now it's time to look at some of the secrets that have helped other CEOs succeed.

2

Eight Secrets of Successful CEOs and Leaders Who Speak Well

"To speak, and to speak well, are two things.
A fool may talk, but a wise man speaks."

—Ben Jonson, British Poet and Dramatist

When it comes to public speaking, speakers must technically speak well, but they must also have substance. They must look and sound like leaders—especially if they're CEOs and executives.

Your first focus must be content. Technical skill alone is not enough. Your first concern should be what you say and then how you can make it clear and compelling. The leaders cited in this chapter provide some guidance on powerful messages. Message is the foundation. Without that, you're just a speaker, not a leader.

Secret 1: Talk About Big Ideas

"He can compress the most words into the smallest ideas of any man I ever met."

—Abraham Lincoln, 16th U.S. President

Every speech, presentation, or other communication needs one big idea. A big idea is all that most people can remember. A big idea has a life of its own. And it doesn't require a big *speech*. It's big because of its *power*, not its *length*.

Abraham Lincoln's Gettysburg Address is 271 words, and it's one of the best speeches ever given. Back on that day in 1863, the crowd hadn't even come to hear President Lincoln; they were there to listen to the country's most famous orator, Edward Everett, who talked for two hours. When Lincoln got up, he gave the address in three minutes. But in three minutes, there was one big idea. He persuaded the nation to fight on. In Appendix E, you can read the speech.

No one likes long speeches. Personally, I never like it when I'm asked to give a forty-five-minute keynote—it's too long! Short speeches, big ideas—that's the secret. Another example of a big idea is President Kennedy's 1961 speech that inspired the United States to put a man on the moon. At the time, the country had fallen behind the Soviet Union in the space race and had made only a few successful manned flights. Kennedy said we would go to the moon, and we did—we landed before the decade was out.

> *We choose to go to the moon. We choose to go to the moon in this decade and do the other things, not because they are easy, but because they are hard, because that goal will serve to organize and measure the best of our energies and skills, because that challenge is one that we are willing to accept, one we are unwilling to postpone, and one which we intend to win, and the others, too.*

Secret 2: Speak in the Moment

No one likes a canned speech. Canned speeches turn people off. You must talk to people about what is happening in the moment. "If you think about the usual setting," said one CEO, "you have an audience sitting there saying, 'Who is this person and why is he talking?' That's not a great setting to start with. It appears somewhat adversarial." Your message must be about them and about what's happening in the moment in order to win over an audience that isn't sure it even wants to listen.

Arnold Zetcher, president and CEO of Talbots, was being honored by the National Retail Federation a few months after the tragedy of September 11, 2001. He knew this particular speech had to be different from the others he had given. He said, "The first draft was a basic acceptance speech, and then we thought, 'Wait a minute, we need to talk about what people are thinking. We need to talk about something bigger. It has to be about the country.'" Zetcher and his team revamped the whole speech, and it was one of the best he had ever given.

When Sovereign Bank was opening its offices in New England, there was a lot of doubt about whether the company could compete with the other banks in the region. Chairman and CEO John Hamill called a meeting of all five hundred employees to erase this doubt. "I decided the only thing I could do was face the questions head on," he said. "The meeting had to deal with what was on their minds, then and there." He talked about why he had joined the bank and why he believed in his heart they would succeed. "Confronting the doubt made it work," he said. "When you are in touch with what people are thinking in that moment, you can confront it and clean it out to get them ready to hear the important message."

Secret 3: Keep It Simple

One problem with many speeches is that they try to do too much. Your message must be simple and straightforward to be remembered.

Roger Marino, founder of the high-tech giant EMC, grew up in a working-class neighborhood on Boston's north shore and got his electrical engineering degree from a co-op school, Northeastern University. Yet, Marino was a salesman at heart. EMC sold one of the least sexy products or services you can imagine—storage systems for computer information—but he and his two partners built a company that went on to dominate the industry.

Marino learned early on how important communication is in business—particularly when it comes to keeping things simple. "When I was in college and I would see one of these engineering professors talking, if I didn't get what they were talking about, it was annoying," he said. "I couldn't figure out why other people thought a professor who couldn't explain things was so brilliant."

Marino considered the brilliant professors to be the ones who could actually communicate the ideas in ways people could understand. "Communication is everything," he said. "You really have to hammer a message home."

Taking his lessons learned in college to the business world, Marino considers the simple message his strength. Keeping it simple is how he keeps people interested and absorbed in the subject at hand—no matter what it is. "I can teach golf or tennis precisely because I *don't* have natural ability. I just explain the steps," he said. "A CEO has to do the same thing: take people from A to B to C."

Secret 4: Be a Straight Shooter

Our survey on communication, discussed in the previous chapter, found that the number one quality that people want in a leader is honesty and integrity. To speak like a CEO, you must have a message that rings true. Audiences want a leader to be more than a good speaker; they want a leader to tell them the truth, no matter what.

Senator John McCain is a straight shooter in politics, where that trait is especially rare. Political leaders have to win votes. They have to please everyone. This tends to keep them from taking a stand. McCain says what he thinks; he doesn't mince words, no matter the consequences. Once in a while, he has succumbed to political pressure, but it doesn't happen often.

The fact that he is a straight shooter helped him during his brief campaign for president in 2000. He told reporters something that wasn't true—that he respected South Carolina's decision to fly the Confederate flag over its statehouse. Later, he explained, "I feared that if I answered honestly, I could not win the South Carolina primary. So, I chose to compromise my principles. I broke my promise to always tell the truth."

McCain had a reputation for telling the truth, so people accepted his apology. This is important for leaders to know. People will accept when you make a mistake. They will not accept the perpetuation of the lie. Every CEO should know that honesty is the secret to winning trust and being a real leader.

A reputation for honesty can take you all the way to the top. Sallie Krawcheck was appointed CEO of Citigroup after the corporate scandals that hurt so many businesses in 2001. Citigroup needed to prove its independence, so it shunned big-league brokerage experience and named Krawcheck for her honest reputation, which she had earned at the independent, boutique investment-research firm Sanford C. Bernstein, first as a top analyst and later as CEO. Krawcheck had actually been dubbed "the Straight Shooter" by *Money* magazine, and *Fortune* magazine's headline about her had said, "In Search of the Last Honest Analyst."

Secret 5: Be an Optimist

"It was the best of times, it was the worst of times."

—CHARLES DICKENS, Author, *A Tale of Two Cities*

When you are the CEO, you face good times and bad, and you must balance reality with hope. A hallmark of leadership is optimism. The CEO must see and talk about what's *possible*.

When Bill Ford Jr. ousted CEO Jacques Nasser at Ford Motor Company in 2001, the company was losing billions of dollars. Morale was low, Ford Motor was getting hammered about quality, and speculation about Ford Jr.'s commitment to run the company surfaced in the press and within the industry.

At a news conference in June 2003 to announce quarterly earnings, reporters were still hammering away at the weaknesses in Ford Motor Company, but Ford Jr. responded to each question with optimism. "We are back on firm footing," he said. "I feel good about where we are today and where we are headed. I am very fired up about the results we are seeing and the products we have coming." In fact, within twenty months, Ford had turned the company around and booked an $896 million profit in the first quarter alone.

Ford Jr. also addressed questions about his commitment to Ford Motor. "This reluctant CEO stuff is for the birds," he said. "It's a privilege and an honor to run this company. There is nothing I would rather be doing."

When Ford Jr. drove away after the news conference, the usual protesters weren't there to greet him. This time, several dozen supporters instead gathered around his Lincoln Navigator. One fan shouted, "Keep up the good work!"

Secret 6: Focus on the Future

"Most of the important things in the world have been accomplished by people who have kept on trying when there seemed to be no hope at all."

—Dale Carnegie, Author, *How to Win Friends and Influence People*

In difficult times, we look to leaders for hope. New York mayor Rudy Giuliani was in midtown Manhattan when the first plane hit the World Trade Center on September 11, 2001. On that morning, his political career was on thin ice; he had been kicked out of the house by his wife, who was furious after publicity about a mistress.

But that day, Giuliani knew what he had to do. First, he went to the scene of the disaster and risked his life—he was trapped in the rubble for fifteen minutes. When he emerged, he went straight out to talk to reporters. When the rest of the world was still trying to figure out what had happened, Giuliani focused on hope. Asked about New Yorkers, he said, "They are just the most wonderful people in the world." He declared, "We have, without any doubt, the best police department, fire department, the best police officers, the best fire officers, the best emergency workers of any place in the whole world."

Giuliani almost immediately turned New York's attention to the future. He said, "The people in New York City will be whole again. We are going to come out of this emotionally stronger, politically stronger, much closer together as a city, and we're going to come out of this economically stronger, too."

Hope is a potent message. Focus on the future and what can be done. When you speak, tell people what you believe is possible. Your vision, your hope, your belief about the future sets the course for the organization. Focus on the future, and people will go out and make it happen.

Secret 7: Be Real

"This above all: to thine own self be true."

—WILLIAM SHAKESPEARE, English Dramatist and Poet, *Hamlet*

A CEO is at a distinct disadvantage with many audiences. Your title puts them off. They believe they have nothing in common with you. This is a lousy way to start a speech, a meeting, or even a conversation. Your job is to find a way to make a connection. To connect, you must be real.

Dan Wolf, founder and CEO of Cape Air, has a reputation for doing this. He is warm, self-effacing, and genuine with audiences. He draws on his background and eclectic interests to connect with audiences. Before he became CEO, he was a political science major who earned his commercial aviation license and became both a flight instructor and a certified mechanic. As you can imagine, in his town meetings with employees, he can relate to individuals—he can talk to pilots as a pilot, to mechanics as a mechanic, to businesspeople as a businessman.

"I use self-effacing humor," he explained. "Physical attributes, like bald jokes, work. And I'm legendary for being more of an entrepreneur than a manager. My organizational skills are not great, and that's great material for humor, too." Good leaders are able to humanize themselves and still maintain their authority.

"People are interested in the person who is leading the organization," he said. "They really want to know your feelings, reactions, and opinions. If you can share that in a self-effacing way—so they don't feel like they are watching an egomaniac, but a real human being—you can really connect with people."

Secret 8: Stand for Something

Our survey results as discussed in Chapter 1 made it clear that people aren't just working for a paycheck. They go to work to be part of something bigger. They want the work to have purpose; they want the organization to have a mission. They want to know that what they do makes a difference in some way.

The person who embodies the mission and purpose of an organization is the CEO. The most successful CEOs are perfectly aligned with the mission and purpose of the organization. Those CEOs stand for something.

Judy George is the founder and CEO of Domain, a retailer of designer home furnishings. Before she launched the business, she was president of Scandinavian Design. The story of her company's launch is a great example of how Judy came to stand for something.

On a Sunday morning in 1985, Judy had a meeting with the CEO of Scandinavian Design, expecting to get his approval on a new deal. He fired her. Judy had invited her friends and family to a big party to celebrate the deal, and instead, she had to go home and tell them this news. While it was a shock, Judy got up the next morning and was already thinking about the future. She decided this was actually the opportunity of a lifetime—to start her own company. By 1998, she had grown from 3 employees to 250, with twenty-three stores and $50 million in sales.

Judy's success became a legend, especially among women entrepreneurs. She had bootstrapped her way up, combining a flare for design with hard work and a tough mind for business. Eventually she sold the company and wrote two books, one of which became a bestseller: *The Domain Book of Intuitive Home Design*. She also spoke frequently to business groups and gave many media interviews, sharing much of her personal story.

Judy is frequently recognized in public; people will come up to her just to say hello or to shake her hand. She attributes the recognition to the simple fact that people know her story—and have known it from the very beginning. The lesson in that is, Judy says, "you have to stand for something." She adds, "That's the best advice I can give anyone. And to do that, you have to be willing to reveal something about yourself—by telling people where you've been and the mistakes you've made. They relate to it. They realize that we're all human."

CEOs and leaders who succeed as speakers don't get to the top because of luck. As you've seen in this chapter, there's more to it than technical skill. The truth is that most leaders who speak well were once beginners, but they became great speakers because they *chose* to be—they made the time, the goals, and the commitment to get there. The same goes for you. Your ability to reach a level of success is your decision—you're as good as you decide to be. The tips in Chapter 3 will help you set your decision in motion.

3

You're as Good as You *Decide* to Be

"All the great speakers were bad speakers first."

—Ralph Waldo Emerson, American Poet and Essayist

Are great leaders, athletes, politicians, and speakers born to greatness, or did they learn the skill? Is it nature or nurture?

As Thomas Edison once said, "Genius is 1 percent inspiration and 99 percent perspiration." All the talent in the world won't take you to the top of the PGA or the business world if you don't decide to do what it takes. With all due respect to Nike for one of the world's greatest slogans, you have to *decide* to "just do it."

Speaking well is *your* decision. It doesn't matter if you were an introverted child or the quiet type in high school. It doesn't matter if you didn't have opportunities to speak early in your career. It doesn't matter if you have a busy schedule or a company that doesn't particularly support your professional development. You are the one who has to decide to be great.

All CEOs who speak well were once average, and many were terrible. Many people would like to be better speakers, but they don't make the decision to do what it takes. The decision sets a chain of events in motion. You find the time. People appear in your life. Opportunities arise.

You may be inspired to make a decision of your own by listening to advice from people who are great at what they do. The knowledge and experience shared in this chapter demonstrate that mastering a skill is mind over matter.

Make It a "Game"

The work of becoming great is not always much fun. Even golf can become a job when you have to do it every day and there is pressure to win. So, you have to make work a game. That's what Tiger Woods did. "I always kept it fun," he said of practicing. "Not necessarily by just going out there and beating balls all day; that gets boring. I like to play games, play situational games."

You can take the same approach to the "speaking game." Make it interesting. Look for opportunities to try something new. Put yourself on the line. Set goals and determine what would make an event interesting for you. Set up your own rules, your own guidelines for success. Do more than meet other people's expectations. Set the bar higher. See what you can accomplish. Make the challenge into a game. There are several ways that I have found to do just that. For example, you can reward yourself for practice time. One weekend at a conference in Miami, I made a bargain with myself: I would get up very early to practice the speech two more times so that I could go to the beach before the afternoon session. Another time, as I was preparing a brand-new communications workshop, I set a date and invited friends to a lunch to let them be my test audience. Setting a deadline, bringing in friends, and making it fun gave me the incentive to complete the curriculum to be ready for a real client engagement.

Think about how you can create rewards and incentives that will inspire you to do the work it takes to be good. All work and no play is not a recipe for success. You have to work hard, but you have to enjoy the journey. Personal incentives are a great way to keep yourself motivated so that you don't feel it's all a big grind.

Say "Yes" to Public Speaking

Many people avoid public speaking if they can. In fact, it's often said that many people are more afraid of public speaking than of death. Whether that is true or not, the excuses I typically hear are that people are too busy or have more important things to do.

You can hand off the speaking roles to others in your organization. But you will be missing important opportunities. When you are the CEO, you are the face and voice of the organization, and people expect you to be standing up at the front of the room. You will never improve if you don't say yes to public speaking.

One CEO I know had been promoted to the job for her hard work and contributions to the business side. She was a high performer who got results. She worked hard and made good decisions. But she was never comfortable with public speaking. When she rose to the position, she decided that rather than expose herself, she would hand off the job to her COO. He was outgoing and enjoyed public speaking. She thought she had found the ideal solution.

At employee events, conferences, and even board meetings, the COO did the lion's share of the presentations. She would kick it off and then allow him to give out the awards, outline the business plan, or facilitate the board discussion. She also avoided speaking to the media, preferring to hand that assignment to her trusty lieutenant or someone else in the company.

You can imagine the effect this had on employees, customers, directors, and the public over time. She was barely on the radar screen. This approach clearly undermined her authority with employees and made people wonder who was really in charge. People respected her work but questioned whether she was really up to being CEO. The company also struggled financially, and it was difficult not to conclude that the public absence of the CEO was a contributing factor.

If you are looking to fill any kind of leadership position, you must say "yes" to public speaking. If you want to be CEO, you might as well start now. Don't wait to learn how to do it until you have to—by then, it's almost too late. A CEO needs to be out front, give the speeches, lead the dialogue, present the awards, and talk to the press. That's the role. Whatever your personal preferences, you have to embrace what is required by the job.

Ask for Help

It isn't always easy to ask for help. You may be accustomed to getting things done on your own. A client in financial services got a big promotion to a senior executive position. One Friday, she found herself in a quandary. She had made a commitment to teach a course, attend several meetings, and entertain a client, but she also had a major presentation to give on Tuesday. She didn't have time to brush her teeth, let alone prepare a major speech.

Picking up the phone to ask my firm for help changed the whole crazy dynamic. She could have tried to do it all, but that would have meant doing everything halfway, including the speech. We delegated or canceled several activities and went to work on the presentation. She gave an outstanding speech. The company wowed the client and won the business.

Reaching out to ask for help may not be easy for you. Many successful people are self-reliant. Self-reliance is good. But don't make the mistake of going it alone. Asking for help is one of the most powerful things you can do. You need the perspective of trusted advisers. You deserve to have help from good people who can support you. Surround yourself with good people, and ask for what you need.

Stretch

It's easy to stay in your comfort zone once you have arrived at a certain point in your career. We are rewarded for what we know. Trying new things may seem unnecessary.

When I launched my business, I thought I might be able to help people with public speaking. I didn't know whether I would be able to build a consulting firm. I had no background in business and no experience as an entrepreneur. As I look back, I realize the greatest thrill has been getting up in the morning not knowing how to do it. I had to learn it all, and along the way, I learned a lot of things about myself. It is exhilarating to get up every day and learn how to be successful at doing something new.

Many of my clients have requested coaching believing they would probably learn something but not expecting to enjoy the process. Then, once they begin to stretch the boundaries and to have a little success, they start to feel the thrill. Even at an advanced point in their careers, they experience growth—and growth is exciting. Stretching builds confidence. It makes work more fun and fulfilling. It provides professional and personal satisfaction. When you push yourself toward learning something new, you see what you are capable of achieving.

A Common Mistake

The CEO of a manufacturing company was passionate about his business, but his presentations were dull and boring. He plodded through the stats and numbers and put people to sleep. The chairman of the board pulled him aside and told him he thought he could do better. The company needed to be energized, and the chairman said it was up to him to connect with people and create the excitement.

We set aside the PowerPoint slides with the graphs and numbers and talked about his successes and disappointments. He had a new plant overseas that was struggling. He wanted to encourage those employees to overcome their obstacles. We talked about their failures and successes, their challenges and goals. We wrote down stories about other employees who had overcome obstacles, and about what he had learned early in his own career.

Now we had stories about hard work and perseverance, stories about innovation and creative approaches. He put together a presentation without graphs and charts. He simply told the stories. The stories told those employees that he knew them and believed in them. The speech was a success. The audience was inspired. The employees went back to work, resolved many of the problems, and turned things around.

Everyone should have the experience of being back on the edge, wondering what he or she is going to learn today. The CEO's decision to stretch made a major impact on his organization. If what you're doing isn't working, try something else. Take risks. Go beyond your comfort zone. You will be rewarded in ways you never imagined.

Invest in Yourself

A leader puts the interests of the company first. Sometimes that makes it difficult to decide to invest in *you*. Investing time and money in developing your skill may not be a line item in your budget. However, it is in fact one of the best investments you can make, because as CEO you are the face and voice of the organization.

A bank executive was a mediocre speaker who often struggled during Q&A sessions without a script. It was tolerated because the executive made other valuable contributions. But after one meeting in which he stumbled badly on questions from the board, the CEO put his foot down. He let it be known that the executive had to get help on presentations.

This was the first time the executive had ever heard this was an issue. He had never thought it necessary to develop his public speaking skill. He assumed that his other contributions to the company would more than make up for lackluster presentations.

Even if no one has ever mentioned it, you owe it to yourself to find out how your skills stack up. If you get an honest assessment of your skills, you will be able to determine how much of an investment to make. You may remember the commercial for hair color in which the actresses say, "Because I'm worth it." All executives, male and female, should have the same attitude about investing in their own professional development. You're worth it.

Invest what it takes to develop your skills. Do it before you hear from your boss that it's a problem. You will never regret the time you spend developing these skills. You will only increase your confidence and become a more effective leader.

Communicate Regularly

Once you become CEO, you can't speak just some of the time. You have to stay out front and be visible. When Charlie Baker became president and CEO of Harvard Pilgrim Health Care, the company was faltering. He decided he had to stay in touch with employees in this tough time.

"I knew it should be steady, understandable, regular communication about what we were doing and why," said Baker. He decided to send an e-mail to employees every Friday, whether the news was good or bad. He was honest about what HPHC was doing to make things better. It worked. "They bought into the notion that we would work things out. That created optimism. It's a major reason why we made it," he said. Soon, employees started to circulate the e-mails to people outside— health care providers, hospitals, and physicians who were also concerned about the future of the company.

"It was amazing," he said. "A lot of people came up to me and told me during that rough period it helped them understand what we were up to. It made it easier for them to stick with us and say good things when the news wasn't always positive."

Baker joined HPHC in mid-1999, the same year the company lost $277 million. He turned the company around in three years. HPHC now has eight hundred thousand members, twenty-two thousand physicians, 125 hospitals, and, as of the end of 2004, has been profitable under Baker's leadership for seventeen consecutive quarters.

Communicating regularly is one of the keys to being effective; the more you do it, the better you get. People expect to hear from you, and they appreciate being in touch with the boss. "It creates a relationship," Baker noted. He still sends the e-mails every Friday. "There are a lot of people who get those in their mailboxes every Friday and tell me they feel a big connection," he said.

Communicating regularly is not only good for your organization but also good for you. It forces you to articulate where you're going and how you're going to get there.

Start Telling Stories

Storytelling is a leadership skill. Telling stories in informal settings—such as around the office, in meetings, or during conversations—makes the occasions more enjoyable and helps you connect with people. Telling stories in formal settings, such as speeches or presentations, helps you make your points without hitting people over the head.

Good stories make for good speeches. Dan Wolf, CEO of Cape Air, grew up in a family that sat around the dinner table telling stories. One of Dan's brothers actually makes a living as a storyteller. Dan brought storytelling to the role of CEO. At one memorable awards luncheon that I attended, he regaled the audience with a hilarious tale about how he explained to his children why he had been named an honorary "Good Guy." He was brilliant—we were hanging on every word, completely engaged by his humor, wit, and storytelling mastery. People weren't just politely listening—they were thoroughly entertained. His stories made the difference.

If you grew up telling stories around the dinner table, you're fortunate, because telling stories will come naturally in your professional life. However, even if you didn't grow up in a storytelling family, you can learn the art. I'm not talking about learning how to repeat a good joke you've heard, although that's nice. This is about telling your own original stories—stories that have a point.

People love stories. Stories are a way of revealing who we are and how we think. Stories allow you to point out behaviors and values without sounding as if you're bragging or giving a lecture. Start by considering stories you have told to friends or family members. You can also start paying more attention to what's going on around you. Once you do, I promise that just about every day you will have at least one story. Storytelling begins with awareness. We'll talk more about storytelling in Chapter 9. In the meantime, if you have lived a life, you have stories to tell, and you can use those stories to communicate effectively.

I once attended a workshop on storytelling with Marcia Reynolds and Vickie Sullivan, speakers and consultants who help professional speakers enhance their skills. I had spent twenty years telling *other people's* stories in television news reports. I was pretty convinced that I hadn't had a very exciting life and didn't have good stories of my own.

Marcia and Vickie showed the group that we all have stories. They suggested that we look for them in the challenges we had faced. They recommended that we reflect on the conflicts we had witnessed or experienced. Sometimes you need a little distance from those conflicts to understand what they meant. Write them down and tell them to your family; explore what they are really about. Stories can be about you or about people you know. Become aware of people and events that could become good stories. Try them out and see where they go. Telling stories can become one of the most valuable tools of a CEO; they're one of the most effective means to communicate your leadership in a way that inspires and motivates listeners.

4

What You Can Learn from Ten Thousand Leaders and Working on TV for Twenty Years

"Experience is the name everyone gives to their mistakes."

—OSCAR WILDE, Irish Playwright

ONE OF THE GREAT benefits of working in television news is that you get to meet and interview a lot of interesting people. In 2003, I was filling in as host of the morning show on a Boston radio station. On Friday as I was leaving the studio, the producer called out that Hillary Clinton might stop in on her book tour the following week. The former first lady's autobiography, *Living History*, was hot off the presses. I hadn't read it yet, but I figured I would check out a few chapters when I returned to work on Monday.

You can imagine my surprise on Monday morning when I arrived at the station at five o'clock and learned that Hillary Clinton would be calling by cell phone from La Guardia Airport—in five minutes. She was available to do the interview at that time only—the rest of her day was booked. Talk about pressure! News reporters are used to working on short deadlines, but this was ridiculous. I hadn't read Chapter 1, page 1, of *Living History*.

This was going to be interesting. We stalled long enough for me to write up three or four questions. I thought about what other people would want to know. I figured that most people listening to the interview hadn't read the book either.

The secret to any interview is to ask the obvious. So, I asked her why she wrote the book, whether she was running for president, and how she felt about her critics. I also asked her to tell us the biggest surprise about becoming a U.S. senator and what she really thought about Monica Lewinski.

She was brilliant—answering every question without hesitation. I found this remarkable because Hillary Clinton couldn't possibly have known what I would ask; there was no preinterview with her or her staff. Yet, she couldn't have handled it better. After years of being on the firing line with the national media, and a tough race for the U.S. Senate, Hillary Clinton knew how to handle any question. She was prepared. She had thought through what reporters would ask and exactly what she would say.

I am fortunate to have had twenty years of experience interviewing business leaders, political leaders, experts, celebrities, and other interesting people. Those years in television news taught me how intense the spotlight can be. Some leaders handle it a lot better than others.

In this chapter, I offer some advice on handling the spotlight. That spotlight can be intense, and not just if your job is on television. Every day, a CEO is in the spotlight. The lessons of this chapter should help every leader manage the glare.

Lesson 1: Expect the Expected

In 1980 when Ted Kennedy announced he was running for president, Roger Mudd sat him down in a famous interview and asked, "Why are you running for president?" Kennedy stammered through the answer, and the result was disastrous to his candidacy. One of the biggest mistakes you can make is failing to expect the expected.

When you're in the spotlight, you cannot afford to assume you are prepared. You should not walk into the room or get on the phone without stopping for at least a moment to think. I'm not talking about the curveballs. I'm talking about the stuff that's obvious. One of the hardest "questions" for authors on book tours to answer is, "Tell me about your book." Equip yourself to handle the basic stuff. You will not get a second chance. People can forgive you if you don't know some little, obscure detail, but they expect you to be ready to handle what's already evident.

George W. Bush didn't give many press conferences in his first term in office, and he wasn't always as prepared as he should have been. But he did learn on the job, and by the time the campaign for his second term had begun, he had become a little more savvy about how to prepare for the press. The day after John Kerry chose John Edwards as his running mate in 2004, a White House correspondent asked Bush the difference between Edwards and Vice President Dick Cheney. "Dick Cheney could be president," answered Bush. "Next?"

By preparing for the basics, you will leave people with the impression that you are "good on your feet." As CEO, whether you're talking to the media, the board of directors, industry analysts on the quarterly call, or employees at an annual meeting, you will get no slack on the obvious. Sometimes when you're busy running from call to meeting to speech, you forget that you need to stop and think it through. The only way to be good is to be very, very well *prepared*.

Lesson 2: If Your Heart Is Beating Fast, It's Usually a Great Opportunity

Not long after Jimmy Carter left the White House, I was working as a television reporter in Philadelphia, when the assignment editor sent me to cover an event at a church in New Jersey where the former president was speaking. We weren't interested in the speech, but we hoped we might get lucky and hear Jimmy Carter's comments on a major news story of the day. Unfortunately, this was hard to do. He did not have press availability before or after the event. In other words, it probably wasn't going to happen.

The pews were already filled, and my photographer and I were heading up the hill to the church, where we would set up in the back. That was when I spotted Jimmy Carter, with no other reporters around, walking with two Secret Service guys. They were about to enter the church. I felt my heart beating fast. I hadn't expected to have this opportunity, and I had not actually prepared a single question. But, this was the moment. We jogged over the grass (I was in heels) and got the former president to give us a one-on-one interview.

Opportunities come along. You can't let a racing heart stop you. You may find yourself standing on stage as a keynote speaker. You may find yourself sitting down to a major media interview. Use anxiety to improve your performance. Seize the moment and ignore the fear. You are about to encounter something big. A racing heart and sweaty palms can be a sign of opportunity.

Lesson 3: Walk on Stage as if You Belong There

Joe Biden was assured reelection to the U.S. Senate by the time election night rolled around in 1984. Since it wasn't a close contest, my assignment editor sent me to Delaware to cover the acceptance speech—an easy job that even I, as the new reporter, couldn't screw up. The top reporters at the station—the ones who get the lead stories—were sent to the big, contested races where there was excitement. Since I was still new, the producer said I probably wouldn't even have to do a live report; they would just take a feed from Biden's acceptance speech for the eleven o'clock news.

Our camera crew set up on the risers designated for the media in the back of the room with the other local stations. Back at the station, all of the reporters at the big races were chatting away through the evening about their stories. However, by eleven o'clock, all the big election results were in. The producers needed something else to put into the newscast. That's when Joe Biden took the podium. The producer keyed the internal microphone that went out to remote locations, and I heard in my ear, "See if you can get Biden live."

This was a bit of a problem. Senator Biden was at least three hundred feet away on stage. A crowd of three hundred and fifty partying Democrats stood between us and the stage. We had not asked in advance for an interview, and already, he was winding up his speech. At any minute, he would disappear from the stage.

I jumped off the riser and made my way through the crowd, but down below the stage I still couldn't get the senator's attention. I realized my only hope was to climb the steps and go up on stage. Acting as if I belonged, I walked straight over to the senator at the podium and touched him on the arm. "Senator Biden, Channel 10 news. I wonder if you would like to speak to us live. Our camera is just over there."

Perhaps my bold move took him by surprise, but he certainly wasn't put off. In fact, he took *me* by the hand and led *me* through the crowd to the bank of cameras in the back. We got him on TV, and the news director was happy because we were the first channel to do so—and all the other stations followed suit. Since I was first to get the interview, it was a coup—my boss started giving me many more interesting political assignments.

As a CEO, you have to always walk on stage as if you belong there. And that means everywhere you go, because the world is your stage. This doesn't mean that you ever appear arrogant or controlling—you simply give the impression that you are comfortable and belong there. Show them you are comfortable in the role. Comfort goes hand-in-hand with confidence and leadership. Even in a new situation, put other people at ease and you will come across like a leader.

Lesson 4: Keep the Worst-Case Scenario in Mind

On April 1, 1985, I learned the hard way that you have to at least consider the worst-case scenario. I was in Philadelphia when Villanova beat out Georgetown to claim the NCAA basketball championship title—a game that is ranked in many polls as the top NCAA upset ever. Don't get me wrong: I was glad Villanova won. But I—just like the rest of the fans—didn't *expect* them to win. And that put me in a dangerous situation.

On the night of the game, our television crew had set up a live truck in the middle of the campus. We were going about our business as the minutes ticked down on the game clock. The game was on in the truck, and we could see that Villanova was still in it. Students inside the dorm rooms were cheering wildly. Still, we didn't *believe* Villanova could win. The game was back and forth down to the wire, and as the last seconds ticked away, students started pouring out. The buzzer rang, and Villanova had won. The Cinderella team had pulled it off.

However, it was now a whole new ball game for our crew. The crowds began swelling around us. No security guards, no police, and no other television stations were anywhere near us. The crowd pressed us closer to the truck until we were pinned against it. All we could do was make our way to the back of the truck, where we could scale a ladder to the top. We scrambled up and set up the camera. The vantage point was great, but when the camera light went on, the crowd went wild and began rocking our truck. We suddenly had visions of capsizing onto a crowd of students.

Fortunately, that didn't happen, and we made it down safely—but what a lesson in how your assumptions can leave you ill-prepared! How does this translate to business? Have a contingency plan. Consider what could happen. Think about all the possible scenarios. This is especially important when you are dealing with the media in a crisis.

Every organization should have a crisis plan that includes media. The plan should stipulate when, where, and how you will communicate with all your stakeholders and the news media, too. I hope you never have to execute the plan, but it is peace of mind to have one. Anticipate the worst and hope for the best. Someday you might be glad you did.

Lesson 5: The Good News Is: There Is Bad News

A colleague of mine, Paula Lyons, the onetime consumer editor for ABC's "Good Morning America," tells the story of interviewing a General Motors executive after a disastrous string of news for the company. Cadillac dashboards were going up in flames because the company had apparently forgotten to install the tops of ashtrays. Rather than make excuses, this guy admitted there was bad news—and he took ownership of the problem.

"What went wrong in the installation?" she asked the spokesperson. "Somebody goofed," he answered. That was that. He answered the question with the unvarnished truth and defused the situation. The rest of the interview focused not on the mistake, but on how GM was going to correct it. My colleague says she wished more people knew how to admit their mistakes and face the music as he did.

Bad news is bad news, but it's also good news if you know how to handle it. Managing the tough questions can actually make your organization look better than before. People accept mistakes if you make an apology. What they hate is avoidance. If you can handle the spotlight during a crisis, people are impressed.

As CEO, you are the person to whom they look in a crisis. Someone has to be in charge. If you see those moments as leadership opportunities, it will change your attitude and help you when you're under pressure.

Of course, people in the media like bad news—because bad news is news. Television ratings skyrocket when bad things happen. People pay attention because something's happening, and they want to know what. Whether it's a blizzard or a terrorist alert, the media know people will tune in for the latest. While bad news may not be good for your business, you can make the best of things by learning to deal with bad news and communicate effectively. As CEO, you can shape new perceptions. You can bring your organization back on course. In Chapter 12, you'll find more information on handling crises.

Lesson 6: Polish Your Professional Image

I grew up in a small town in the Midwest where there wasn't a large Irish population. Saint Patrick's Day in our town was no big deal—it certainly wasn't a *real* holiday with parades and time off from work as it is in places such as Boston. So, I had never worn green on Saint Patrick's Day.

This was a problem on March 17, 1988, when I was anchoring WBZ-TV 4 in Boston. I went to work dressed in an orange suit. That night, when the five o'clock news started, the station's phones rang off the hook. Apparently, without knowing it, I had offended countless Irish Catholics who find the color orange offensive.

I later learned that orange is associated with Northern Irish Protestants because of William of Orange, the king of England, Scotland, and Ireland who, in 1690, defeated the deposed King James II, a Roman Catholic, in the fateful Battle of the Boyne, near Dublin. Green is the color of the Irish Catholic nationalists of the south—think shamrocks and verdant landscapes—and also revolution.

My Saint Patrick's Day in orange was quite a donnybrook. After the newscast, when the phones had finally stopped ringing, the assistant news director called me in. "What were you thinking?" she asked. "Don't you understand where you are? This is Boston!"

Image is important, and so is symbolism. You must fit in and be appropriate wherever you go. Your sensitivity to knowing what to say and do is critical. Dress appropriately, and know the customs and culture wherever you go. If you don't know, buy a book or ask someone. This is important whether you travel internationally or just to a different neighborhood. Exhibiting familiarity with people and their ways is a sign of respect.

Image is important even on your own turf. Your office, conference room, and surroundings are all part of image. Likewise, your outfit and your accessories matter, from your suit to your briefcase, pen, and shoes.

Senior executives must understand the language of clothing in the business world. They must have a wardrobe that works well for all types of events they attend. Whether your office is business-casual or more formal, you set the tone and have to be on your game. Consistency of image is important. Even if you are accustomed to shopping for your wardrobe, you may want to get assistance from a wardrobe consultant or personal shopper. You rarely will get honest feedback about your clothing from people you know because the subject is so personal. People will tell you they like something you are wearing when they don't. The best way to dress like a CEO is to get someone with a good eye to help you.

Lesson 7: Know When Enough Is Enough

Occasionally in television, consultants come in to review tapes of newscasts and provide outside advice on how to improve the program. A colleague of mine who was on the air had a more endearing term for them—she called them the "insultants." It isn't always a pleasant experience for the on-air "talent," but sometimes, I have to admit, they have a valuable perspective.

In one memorable but painful critique, the consultant suggested that our team needed to cut the chitchat. "How much should we cut?" asked my coanchor Joe Shortsleeve. "Cut it in *half*," replied the consultant. Joe and I looked at each other and laughed. We had no idea we were that annoying. We were entertaining each other and thought the audience must be having fun, too.

For months after that, we had good laughs with each other about the advice. "Cut it in half" became our mantra, but it worked—we got the hint. What's the message for anyone in the spotlight? When you are on stage, don't get carried away with the sound of your own voice.

CEOs must learn to turn on their own "internal editor." You must know when enough is enough. The advice I give clients is: When you get to the point where you wonder, "Am I talking too much?" the answer is that you probably are. A CEO should give crisp, clear answers to questions; don't belabor a point or talk just because the microphone is yours. Be respectful of people's time and their ability to get your gist. Don't repeat yourself. Watch their eyes: if they are glazing over, stop.

For a leader, every day is a day in the spotlight, but you can manage the glare if you prepare yourself for it. It's important to prime yourself for all situations—good or bad, new or routine—because they *will* happen. Regardless of the situation, if you show that you're comfortable in your role through confidence, preparation, and polish, your leadership ability will shine through.

5

The Eight Most Frequent
Mistakes People Make
in Front of Crowds and Cameras

"Only the prepared speaker deserves to be confident."

—DALE CARNEGIE, American Author and Trainer

IN THIS CHAPTER, you will learn from the mistakes CEOs and other leaders have made in front of crowds and cameras. These top eight mistakes will show you what to avoid in the spotlight—but also help you see what it takes to be successful.

Mistake 1: Underestimating the Importance of Public Speaking to Your Career

A retail executive had been promoted to CFO. She had a strong financial background and a seventeen-year track record. She had earned the CEO's respect for her candor and hard work. However, because she'd been overseas for several years, she didn't know her U.S. colleagues well.

In the first weeks in her new stateside position, she uncovered problems in her operation and quietly went to work. She was not someone who sought the limelight or asked for help. She also avoided making presentations and was quiet in meetings unless someone asked her a question.

While that approach may have worked for her in the past, it was about to backfire now. Senior leaders in this particular organization expected to help each other by sharing information. E-mails leaked out about her problematic operational situation, and the senior team confronted her. The CEO scheduled a meeting, and she was asked to make a PowerPoint presentation.

A crisis is no time to learn how to make a good presentation. The new executive not only had to put together her slides and prepare her talk but also knew she had to get ready to face some tough questions. Fortunately, she pulled a lot of people in to help. She practiced and prepared. She delivered a decent presentation. And she learned an important lesson. "It took seven years off my life," she said. "I realized this is something I should have learned a long time ago."

Don't wait—your time will come. If you want to lead the company, you should never underestimate the importance of public speaking. You will be judged by the way you handle the hot seat. The judgment day isn't six months before they decide to make you CEO. Judgment days happen all along the way. Be ready long before you have to be ready.

Mistake 2: "Winging" Important Speeches, Presentations, or Media Interviews

A top division president in a large company was regarded as the number one candidate in the CEO succession plan. In three years, he would have the opportunity to take over a great company. He had run several of the company's divisions and earned the respect of his subordinates as well as his colleagues and boss.

One day, he was asked to give a presentation to the company's entire leadership group. He was busy with several other business issues and put little time into the presentation, figuring he could wing it. He knew everything there was to know about the business and often gave employee presentations. What did he really need to do to prepare?

The presentation was poor—meandering and disjointed. He annoyed the rest of the group. They liked him but wondered whether his inability to focus and make a clear presentation was a sign he was not up to the job of CEO. The company's head of professional development put him into coaching with my firm, and we tried scheduled one session. However, after the first session, he found reason after reason to cancel the second. We didn't see him again.

The same day this promising executive gave a lousy presentation, the president of another division had given a great talk. He not only had done his homework but also spoke with clarity, appeared well organized, and answered questions with ease. A year later, when the first executive was asked to move down to a small subsidiary, this executive moved into the succession plan. It had all come down to one presentation. It may be unfair, but that's the real world.

Winging a presentation is a bad idea most of the time. Not many people can do it. Even if you are comfortable in front of an audience, your presentation must be organized, and your points must be crisp. Don't get me wrong: there are times and places when you have to or should wing it. You should be good on your feet, but you should never go into a formal presentation without preparation. You should think about what you want to say, prepare, and practice. At the CEO level, clarity is king. Respect yourself and your audience by taking time to think it through before you get there.

Mistake 3: Leaving It All to the Speechwriters

When a Wall Street executive became president of his college, he hired a talented speechwriter to join his staff. Her first project was the new president's inaugural address to faculty, alumni, students, family, and friends. This speech would not only launch his term as president but also set a new direction for the college. Since he was not a traditional academic, this speech was even more important.

The first version of the speech was a good overview of the history and tradition of the school. The writer had done an excellent job of stating the accolades the school had received, the school's strengths, and some of the blueprints for future development. However, as we sat back and listened to the president read this speech, his speechwriter and I realized something was missing. What was missing was the president himself. He was not in his own speech. We weren't learning why he was there, what made him tick, or what were his personal reasons for taking this important job.

The speechwriter and I decided to go back to the drawing board, turn on the tape recorder, and interview the president. Among the many things we learned was that although he had graduated from the college and served on the board, he had not been an A student. In fact, he joked that he had been an average student at best.

We decided that a personal fact wasn't just an aside—it was an opportunity to connect with the audience. Tapping into his genuine humility and humor helped us craft the opening few remarks in a whole new way. We would not hide the fact that he wasn't an academic—we would highlight it to help him connect with the audience and be himself. Here's an excerpt:

> As I look around, I see many familiar faces—even friends dating back forty years to when I was an undergraduate. Some of you may be surprised to see me standing here today as president. As a matter of fact, the Search Committee called the chief marshal and the only faculty member from my student years, and he has confirmed that I graduated in good standing. I hope he pointed out that I was in the top 50 percent of my class.

If you leave every aspect of speechwriting to a speechwriter, even the best writer in the world will not capture you. It takes years of working with a speechwriter to be able to just hand it all over. *You* must be in your own speeches—and that means you must work with the speechwriter. You can't expect writers to work that magic without your help.

If you can hire a good speechwriter, you should. Good speechwriters are invaluable. Every CEO needs someone inside or outside the organization to help with the sheer volume of presentations that are on the calendar. It's good to find someone who thinks the way you do and who understands your philosophy and values, as well as your pace, rhythm, timing, and unique way of expression. But you will always give a better speech if you work with the speechwriter to make it yours. Make it a point to be in your own speeches, and don't expect other people to dig it up. Give the access. Answer questions. Offer ideas. Get involved. You will get what you deserve: a speech that sounds as if it's coming from you.

Mistake 4: Not Answering the Question

In 2002, in a contentious debate with her Republican opponent for governor of Massachusetts, Democrat Shannon O'Brien drove the audience crazy . . . and not in a good way. As the *Boston Globe* reported, "O'Brien seemed to be unwilling or unable to answer a question about whether, if elected, she would veto a large tax increase." The newspaper quoted voters who were watching on television monitors with the reporter from the newspaper. They were exasperated: "'She doesn't want to answer it!' Todd King, a recently laid-off biotech worker, said to the television. 'I don't think she's answered one question yet,' agreed Heather Lee, 27, a Libertarian. 'She's still not answering!' King exclaimed a few minutes later."

By contrast, undecided voters said the opponent, Mitt Romney, answered all the questions, and "all the dirty laundry she tried to hang, he basically cleared it all up," according to one. The media polls began to turn after that debate. Republican Mitt Romney won the race, despite the fact that the vast majority of Massachusetts's voters are liberal and tend to be either Democrats or independents.

You need to answer the questions. Answer honestly, even if it's not what everyone wants to hear. Candor is essential to leadership whether you are running for office or running a company. Take tough questions head on. Earn the respect of your audience, even if you know they will disagree with you.

One of the best and most often quoted movie lines ever written was spoken by Jack Nicholson's character, Colonel Nathan Jessup, in *A Few Good Men*: "You can't handle the truth!" But I will respectfully disagree.

People can handle the truth. Not answering the question is a surefire way to get into hot water.

Mistake 5: Forgetting the Audience

"When people see us, they must know we are worthy of their time."

—FLORENCE LITTAUER, Professional Speaker

I was called to jury duty on a day in May that happened to be National Law Day. A court officer briefed the jury pool on the selection process and then herded us into a large courtroom across the street. Law Day ceremonies were getting under way, and we were not given a choice: we had to attend. Yet, as we filed in, we found there were few open seats because "honored guests" and school students were there. Someone finally brought in some makeshift chairs for two hundred of us in the back of the room. One court clerk actually suggested that I stand for the next hour, but I insisted on having a chair.

For ninety minutes, the ceremony dragged on. The chief justice of the trial court, the Law Day Committee members, the chair of the House Ways and Means in the Senate, and others all had a turn to pontificate on the importance of Law Day. Each of these speakers acknowledged everyone in the room—judges, legislators, administrators, and students—except us. Not a single one mentioned us. While those who were acknowledged were either students or paid to be there, the jury pool of businesspeople and citizens were taking time from their jobs and their lives, and not one speaker had the courtesy to even thank us for attending.

You cannot speak and be lacking in common courtesy. You must never, ever forget your audience. Your audience has given up time to sit and hear you talk. You cannot give them back their time. You can only thank them for giving it up and make it worth their while. As a speaker, you have an obligation to use their time well.

Focus on your audience. Whether you're speaking to colleagues, customers, or employees, think about them before you write the first word of your speech. In the case of employees, remember that your company is paying them to be there and that time is valuable. If you waste your employees' time, you waste *your* resources. You can't afford to let that happen.

The best way to make sure you remember the audience is to find out what they want to know. Make a call, talk to some people who know the audience, and learn how your talk could be valuable to them. Do your homework and you will be appreciated for valuing your listeners' time and making the event worthwhile.

Mistake 6: Blowing the Easy Questions

As noted in Chapter 4, Ted Kennedy blew the interview of his presidential campaign when Roger Mudd asked, "Why are you running for president?"

Many people are least prepared for the first slam-dunk question. As a television host, I would sometimes start interviews by saying, "Tell me about your book," and then I'd watch knowledgeable experts stumble through the first response.

You must be ready for the easy, obvious questions. Think about what they will be, and prepare an answer so you get started on the right foot. You may need to bring someone else in to remind you what the obvious questions will be, someone who knows the audience or media outlet. Then, once you have the questions in mind, come up with the big answer. Keep it simple. Don't overwhelm them with detail. No one wants to know how the watch is made; all that matters is that it works. If you're ready for the easy questions, the hard ones will go a whole lot better.

Mistake 7: Not Knowing When to Hold 'em and When to Fold 'em

"Be sincere, be brief, be seated."

—FRANKLIN D. ROOSEVELT, 32nd U.S. President

Teresa Heinz Kerry was supporting her husband, John Kerry, on the presidential campaign trail and was invited to accept an award from a women's political organization. She was briefed several times by her staff that the organization wanted a short talk—no more than seven to eight minutes. The awards ceremony included six other winners, a reception, and a dinner where she would speak. But the staff was reportedly concerned because Teresa Heinz Kerry was notorious for going long.

Sure enough, in spite of the admonitions from her staff, she came to the podium—after 8:30 on a weeknight—and spoke for forty minutes. Her meandering talk, punctuated by whispers and flips of the bangs in her face, had glimmers of interesting topics, but no focus. The audience practically stampeded to the doors. Unfortunately for the Heinz Kerry staff, there were reporters in the room. Here's an excerpt from the *Boston Herald's* Inside Track column:

> *How do you solve a problem like Teresa? We speak of course, of first lady wannabe Teresa Heinz who AGAIN went off the reservation and AGAIN gave a rambling, bizarre speech.*
>
> *"It was endless, pointless and confusing," said one politically connected chick. "And it was far, far too technical as a dinner speech. I mean, the Latin names of drugs? There was an exodus out the door before dessert."*
>
> *Ooh, tough crowd. And there was chocolate mousse on the menu!*

Amen to Kenny Rogers, who sings in "The Gambler," "You gotta know when to hold 'em, know when to fold 'em." There are few things more annoying than a speaker who doesn't know when to sit down. No one wants to invite a longwinded speaker who is unaware of his or her own tendencies. Word always gets around.

How do you quit while you're ahead? First, time your speech by standing up and delivering it—not by sitting and reading, which takes less time. When you get into the room, be ready to improvise. Tune in to the crowd. If your sixth sense tells you that you have been up there too long, you probably have. Pay attention if someone approaches the podium and starts to give you the eye. Few people will criticize you for giving a speech that is too short.

Mistake 8: Forgetting the Humor

Humor is an integral part of public speaking when you are a CEO. Humor loosens up the audience and gives you the opportunity to connect as a real person. The audience doesn't expect you to be David Letterman; you just need to have a little fun and connect with them.

Speaking of David Letterman, he has a great formula: the Top Ten. Many speakers have borrowed it over the years and adapted it to their own topics. This is perfectly acceptable. Borrowing techniques is fine, especially if you are not a professional comedian. The best humor is original humor, but it doesn't have to be labor intensive. Here's an example of how I used a Letterman Top Ten technique to start off a meeting with 1,200 businesswomen. I was the emcee; the keynote speaker was Ann Moore, CEO of Time, Inc. The sponsor was Bank of America, represented by Anne Finucane. The award winner was Nancy Connolly. Those are important facts as you read through the "customized" Top Ten.

Top Ten Reasons Everyone Should Attend the Breakfast for Champions

10. At this hour, the commute to Boston is what it used to be in 1953.
9. It beats whatever chaos is going on at *home* right now.
8. First opportunity to *sit down* and have a real breakfast in 3.5 months.
7. Excuse to tell the boss, "I'll be in after 10 this morning."
6. Opportunity to see how women like Ann Moore, Anne Finucane, and Nancy Connolly *really* look at 7 A.M.
5. Two words—power networking.
4. Free coffee refills.
3. Need to find out how to build and run a multibillion-dollar company.

2. Feel better when I check out tablemates and realize I'm not the only one who hasn't had time for a manicure.

1. What the heck, it's Friday!!!

Speaking is a lot like horse racing—you have to get off to a good start. Don't forget the humor. You don't have to be brilliant. Audiences want to laugh, and they want to have fun. Don't be afraid to give humor a try.

Fortunately for you, the mistakes in this chapter have already been made! Now you have the chance to learn from them. But keep in mind that nobody's perfect—everyone makes mistakes. The key is to identify the lesson in every mistake. You don't have to be a perfect speaker to be successful, but you do have to be *prepared*.

6

The Authenticity Gap: Why the Real You Must Shine Through

"What we're all striving for is authenticity,
a spirit-to-spirit connection."

—OPRAH WINFREY, Talk Show Host

JACK WELCH SHOOK UP the culture of GE and became one of the most admired CEOs throughout the world, and a large part of his success was the fact that people regarded him as authentic. Welch grew up as the son of an Irish American railroad conductor, and he was known to be brutally honest and outspoken. In his autobiography, *Jack, Straight from the Gut*, Welch indicates that when he got promoted, he considered conforming to corporate norms. As a newly minted vice chairman, he showed up at one of his first board meetings wearing a perfectly pressed blue suit, along with a starched white shirt and crisp red tie. A longtime colleague approached Welch after the meeting, touched the perfectly tailored suit, and said, "Jack, this isn't you. You looked a lot better when you were just being yourself."

What Is Authentic?

"The secret of success is sincerity. Once you can fake that, you've got it made."

—JEAN GIRAUDOUX, French Diplomat, Dramatist, and Novelist

Jean Giraudoux had a pretty cynical view. As Abraham Lincoln said, "You may fool all the people some of the time; you can even fool some of the people all the time; but you can't fool all of the people all the time."

Who really wants to fake it? You never get away with it, anyway. It's too much work. And people have intuition. "You can't fake it," says Talbots CEO Arnold Zetcher. "Audiences know when you're being real."

Look up *authentic* in *Webster's* and you'll find something like "genuine, or known to be true." When you *authenticate* something, such as a painting or an antique, you determine that there is evidence of origin and value. Leaders who are authentic project something genuine about themselves. They aren't afraid to let people see who they really are.

"Even the best CEOs have a difficult time in front of an audience," says Peter Rollins, who hosts the ultimate power lunch: the Chief Executive Club of Boston College. The organization gets top-shelf CEO speakers such as Ted Turner, Richard Branson, and Peter Lynch. "It's trite, but the only way to be authentic is to be yourself, as long as you have the content. Instead of being an actor, just be you," Rollins suggests.

The Authenticity Gap

Leaders who can't be themselves in front of an audience have an authenticity gap. An authenticity gap is a real problem for a leader. If you don't appear or sound genuine, people pick up on it and tend not to trust you or listen to what you have to say.

The authenticity gap creates a disconnect between a leader and the audience. The audience doesn't buy it, so the leader has a hard time building real relationships. People don't like or trust people who don't seem genuine.

How do you close the gap? If you're from Texas, you talk like a Texan. If you're a bank CEO, you wear a conservative suit. If you're a family person, you put photos of the kids on your desk. There is no formula; you just have to let a little of you shine through.

CEOs come in all backgrounds and personas; the authenticity is to allow people to "see" that background and persona. And you have to be consistent. You have to let them "see" the same thing all the time. You shouldn't be a chameleon or adapt your persona to an audience; you only need to adapt *your message* to the *interests* of the audience.

The best advice in absolutely any situation is to be you. If you have a hearty laugh, then laugh. If you love loafers, wear them. If you would rather play squash than golf, then don't play golf. Being you always works. Being somebody else never does. To be authentic, you have to bring *yourself* to the role of CEO.

It also helps to give everything your personal touch. Your office, your clothing, the way you entertain or do an event should all be yours. If you're buying a desk, make it your taste. If you like barbecue, serve that when you entertain at home. Authenticity is about honoring your uniqueness and sharing it with others.

One CEO says, "What works for me is to have my stuff around the office—family pictures, and model cars on top of the filing cabinets because people know I like NASCAR. . . . If people know something about you, they feel you are genuine, and it makes everything you do more believable."

"Our character is what we do when we think no one is looking."

—H. JACKSON BROWN JR., Author, *Life's Little Instruction Book*

What People Really Think

Have you ever noticed that people don't always say what they really think? I was riding up on an elevator to a fancy downtown lunch with a well-dressed professional man who appeared to be in his sixties. A young woman in extremely tight black pants, three-inch heels, and a low-cut red satin blouse stepped on at a middle floor. He smiled in her direction.

"That's quite a stunning outfit," he said. She gave him a big smile back. But when she exited at the next floor, and the elevator door closed, he turned to me and looked stricken. "I didn't really mean that," he said. "She looked like a tramp. How could a woman dress like that in a professional office building?"

People rarely tell you what they really think, unless you insist. When you're the boss and you've just given a presentation, some will say, "Great job," and then they'll slice and dice the speech when you're out of sight. People won't risk candor if there is nothing in it for them. So, if you want to know, you have to ask and show that you really want to know.

Our research found that there are certain behaviors and qualities associated with authenticity. Among those are the ability to share information about yourself, including challenges you have faced, your roots, your interests, and your beliefs and values. Candor and consistency are also important qualities. The remaining part of this chapter offers insights on the qualities and behaviors that make a CEO authentic.

Share Your Beliefs

"What is authentic is what you really believe," says John Hamill, chairman and CEO of Sovereign Bank of New England. "I think what works is when you are excited about what you are saying. It isn't just the idea, but the emotion behind the idea, that makes you successful."

Audiences know when you are saying what you really believe, and when you believe what you're saying. All the acting in the world won't convince people if you are not speaking your truth.

As noted in Chapter 2, Senator John McCain is that rare breed of politician who say what they believe without regard to whether what they say will be popular. McCain rarely puts his finger in the wind. He calls them as he sees them. His candor has earned him enormous respect. McCain's ability to speak the truth has helped him make many friends in both parties, which is probably why he has cosponsored a number of bipartisan bills. It was rumored that President Bush, a Republican, and Senator John Kerry, a Democrat, both asked McCain to be on their tickets in 2004. Even Americans who don't agree with McCain's politics wished there were more like him around.

What do you really believe in or feel passionate about? It doesn't hurt, once a year, to take time to write down the things that really matter to you. Your beliefs are your core, and when you allow others to see those inner beliefs, you win friends and build trust. Sharing your beliefs is one of the most authentic things you can do.

Talk About Your Values

We also spoke earlier about Mitt Romney, the Republican venture capitalist and Mormon who became governor of Democratic Massachusetts. How did Romney win over Massachusetts? He talked about his values, and he connected with the values of the voters.

Romney promised to balance the budget during a fiscal crisis, and he did, despite howling from the largely Democratic legislature. In the face of constantly negative newspaper editorials and carping from mayors, sheriffs, and town governments, Romney never wavered from fiscal discipline. He continued to talk about his values. He told one reporter in a magazine profile, "I don't worry about being liked. The most important thing in life is not being liked. The most important thing is being true to who you really are."

Sharing your values is a surefire way to build bridges. People prefer a leader with the courage to talk about convictions over one who says what everyone wants to hear. This is true in politics and business. It's really pretty simple: express your values, and act on your values, and people will respect you and believe that you are genuine.

Be Candid

Colin Powell has won over presidents and world leaders with his candid, no-holds-barred advice. Powell rose to leadership early on with a reputation for candor. Years before he became secretary of state, back when

President George H. W. Bush was considering action against Manuel Noriega in 1989, Powell made an unequivocal recommendation. "We take down Noriega, we take the whole Panamanian defense force, and we restore democracy," Powell proposed. Every administration has always known Colin Powell would speak his mind.

Candor is essential to authentic leadership. You have to speak your mind. You have to convey your opinion without pretty language and qualifiers. Authenticity is about truth. Truth requires candor. Leaders know when and how to use candor, and they don't avoid it.

Reveal Professional Challenges

Judy George, founder and CEO of Domain, learned how important it is to reveal her professional challenges to audiences. On book tours, she began to notice that "people simply want to know what you're all about," she said. "I don't think people enjoy hearing *speeches*," said Judy. "You need to tell people about your mistakes and talk about all the successes that came about from that painful period."

But why share so much? Why risk that sort of vulnerability? Judy explains, "You become authentic to them when you spell out in detail the lessons learned along the way. It's not about being a great speaker. When I go to hear someone speak, I want to be inspired; I want to know the real stuff and the secrets so I can interpret it and bring it into my life."

Be Consistent

Howard Dean's presidential campaign was on fire before a fateful day in Iowa in 2004. After losing the primary, he gave the "I Have a Scream" speech, raising the real Howard Dean. The speech was inconsistent with voters' earlier impressions of a physician governor who was passionate but not angry. The night after the speech, I had the opportunity to be interviewed as part of a panel of analysts, and the topic was "What next for Howard Dean?" Three of us on the panel agreed even that night that it was over. Dean would never recover. "But Dean's campaign is a steamroller. Don't you think he can come back?" the host pushed several times. We shook our heads. "Not a chance," said one of my colleagues. "A speech like that—you're toast."

Inconsistency is the Achilles' heel of political leaders, and business leaders can learn from them. Al Gore suffered from the inconsistency issue, too. Voters couldn't figure out who he really was. Gore's family and friends insisted he was warm and funny, but to the public he seemed wooden and stiff. When he briefly emerged to test the waters for 2004, the confusions continued; he was sporting a beard and pounding the podium with his fists.

When people see something significantly "different" about you, they tend to question all that they believe they know. You have to be consistent. Consistency is reassuring. The world is too unpredictable. Leaders should not be.

Share

What about you is appropriate to share with others when you are a CEO? Certainly you don't want to make people uncomfortable. Beyond that, you can share quite a bit. That means you don't always have to be a CEO. You need to be a person. You need to share a little bit about you, beyond who you are on the job.

Corporate life can be consuming. Intense demands give us less time for personal pursuits. It's important to get in touch with yourself. This isn't about being authentic. It's about having a healthy personal life. Family and friends, interests, travel, entertainment, hobbies, and sports are all important. When you're *living* a life, you are not only a better person but also a person to whom others relate and someone they want to know.

CEOs who make time for friends and family, leisure activities, vacations, sports, reading, entertainment, and fun are able to connect with others. One CEO ran for selectman in his town and won. He didn't have time, but he did it anyway. Those who know him well say he did it because he genuinely believes in family, community, and living a well-rounded life. This aspect made his admirers appreciate him even more.

Living a life is not a three-month project. It's a journey. Make time to bring old or new people and interests back into your life. Stay in touch with friends. Meet new people. Go to new places. Get off the treadmill and relax. Make a list of things you would like to do before you die, and start doing them. And share what you're doing with others.

Honor Your Roots

Another way to connect authentically with others is to honor your roots — to be the person you have always been. You are a product of your hometown, family, friends, schools, previous jobs, and places you've lived. If you leave it all behind, you lose touch with an integral part of you. That's why it helps to reconnect from time to time with the people and places you've known.

Recently I went to a high school reunion, and it was a lot of fun. Although I had not seen most of my classmates in ten years, I was reminded of how much fun I had in high school. I don't know if I had ever appreciated so much as I do now that I'm a little older how my life was shaped by growing up in that small Midwest town. It was not idyllic, but no one's childhood is. No matter the circumstances, those people and experiences molded me.

Getting in touch with the people and places in your life is a wonderful way to rediscover yourself. It helps you understand yourself, as well as connect with other people in a real way.

Have Fun

One of the best CEO speakers I've ever heard is Richard Branson of Virgin Management Ltd. His larger-than-life persona fills a room, and audiences love stories he tells about his business and life adventures. From racing hot-air balloons to building his airline and other companies, Branson enjoys life, and it's one of the reasons for his success. People are attracted to the fun. "Richard Branson was a pleasure to work with," says Peter Rollins, of the Chief Executive Club of Boston College. "I saw the who's who of CEOs lined up to get an autograph from him after his speech." Branson makes speaking, like everything else, fun. You can tell he enjoys recounting stories and talking to people.

Having fun is one of the best means to connect in a real way. You don't have to race hot-air balloons to have some fun and share it with others. Having fun also attracts fun people into your life—employees, colleagues, mentors, investors, and everyone else important to you in business. Believe it or not, you're not just put on this earth to work! You are here to discover yourself and connect with others, and you can do both by having more fun.

Remember, leaders are authentic when they project genuine, bona fide qualities that tune other people in to what they're really like. You're creating valuable connections by honoring your uniqueness and sharing it with others. So, don't be afraid to let a little of you shine through—you will win trust and respect from colleagues, clients, audiences, and employees with your authenticity.

Taking Stock: How Do Your Skills Add Up?

"Setting a goal is not the main thing. It is deciding how you will go about achieving it and staying with that plan."

—Tom Landry, Former Dallas Cowboys Coach

Taking stock is a vital first step in your plan. You can learn to speak well, but first, you must learn how well you speak. Taking stock of your skills will help you determine where you are and where you want to be. As Tom Landry says, setting a goal is not the main thing; it's deciding how to achieve the goal—and to do that, you need to assess your situation.

So, it's time to take stock of your communication skills. How do they add up? What do you do well, and what would you like to improve? Each of us is different. Each of us has strengths as well as areas that need improvement. I have never coached anyone who did not have strengths. It's essential to recognize these strengths and preserve them as you work on the needs you identify. The Six-Step Process in this chapter will help you discover both.

The purpose of the Six-Step Process is to create a kind of balance sheet, with your assets on one side, liabilities on the other. This balance sheet will give you a more complete picture. Once you have this self-assessment, you will be able to create a personal coaching plan.

Why Go Through the Six-Step Process?

The Six-Step Process may seem lengthy and perhaps unnecessary. You may feel like skipping this chapter and just going straight to work. I encourage you to take a little time to go through this so you fully appreciate everything about your communication style.

A few years ago, I enrolled in a public speaking class. Although I had been on television for twenty years and had many opportunities to emcee events or give speeches over the years, I knew I had a lot to learn. My speeches were dull. I didn't know how to fix them. So, I signed up for the class.

When I arrived for the class, I saw that the instructor had a video camera set up in the corner. My heart started beating faster, and my palms got sweaty. I was not prepared to give my speech on *videotape*. However, once I had a chance to review it, it opened my eyes. Several problems were obvious. In addition, with feedback from the coach, I understood how to fix them. I would not have known what to do had I not gone through that videotape assessment process.

Self-assessment is extremely important for any communications coaching program. If you have a coach, the coach can help you. But if you don't have a coach, you can still get a good picture of where you stand by using a video camera and the work sheets and questionnaires provided in this chapter.

The Six-Step Process
1. Tape-record a speech or presentation either live or in a practice session.
2. Review the videotape on your own using the Videotape Work Sheet provided.
3. Ask a coach or trusted adviser to watch the tape and assess it.
4. Complete the Personal Assessment Questionnaire, writing out the answers.
5. Ask friends/colleagues to complete the Trusted Adviser Survey.
6. Create your Personal Balance Sheet, writing down strengths and needs.

Step 1: Tape-Record a Speech or Presentation Live or in a Practice Session

Coaches often videotape and/or record audio of a speech or presentation so they can show their clients what they see. But you can also record the video of a speech, presentation, media interview, or even client meeting or Q&A session.

If you are not comfortable videotaping a real presentation, you can record a practice session. If you do this, just remember to act as if you have an audience in the room; go to the front, start the speech, speak clearly, make eye contact, and smile as if people are there in the room with you.

Be sure you set up the camera close enough so that you can hear the audio when you play it back. You want to know not just how you look but also how you sound.

If you have someone who can help you record the video, even better. An operator can move the camera and follow you if you move around. The operator can also zoom in to get a closer look at your facial expression, or zoom back to get a better view of how you stand and use gestures. Be sure to record a complete presentation so you can evaluate everything about the content and style.

Step 2: Review the Videotape

Before you sit down to review the videotape, take a look at the following content and style guidelines. These checklists will guide you as you make notes about the presentation.

As you play back the tape, use the Videotape Work Sheet on page 71 to make notes about your presentation. On the left, write down "What I like." On the right, jot down "What needs work." Be honest and really look at what you don't like. This is not meant to make you feel bad; it's meant to provide you with a complete picture. Most people end up with a longer "needs work" column on the right side. That's OK. Be sure to write down your strengths, too, so we can build on those.

Some people find it painful to watch a video of themselves. Clients who have never seen themselves on video are usually surprised or even shocked at what they see. But once you get over the initial surprise, you'll see how valuable it is. You will get accustomed to watching yourself. Remember, this is how the rest of the world sees you.

Content Guidelines
___ Interesting opening that gets attention
___ Effectively sets tone, mood, and expectations
___ Clear, compelling ideas or concepts
___ Organized material
___ Conversational
___ No jargon
___ Colorful words
___ Strong vocabulary
___ Descriptive phrases
___ Focuses on audience interests
___ Valuable information
___ Good stories and anecdotes
___ Interesting, relevant facts
___ Good use of humor
___ Current events or news
___ Effective handouts or visuals

Style Guidelines
___ Posture
___ Eye contact
___ Smile
___ Facial expression
___ Body language
___ Movement
___ Gestures
___ Attire and grooming
___ Hairstyle
___ Accessories
___ Makeup (if applicable)
___ Energy and enthusiasm

_____ Comfort level
_____ "Belongs" on stage, owns the space
_____ Voice quality
_____ Inflection
_____ Tone
_____ Pace
_____ Pronunciation/diction/accent
_____ Effective pauses
_____ No vocal habits (*um, uh*)
_____ Phrasing

Step 3: Ask a Coach or Trusted Adviser to Review the Videotape

Next, you will ask a coach or trusted adviser to review the video (or watch a real presentation). Make a copy of the Videotape Work Sheet for your

▪ Videotape Work Sheet

What I Like	What Needs Work
1. _____	1. _____
2. _____	2. _____
3. _____	3. _____
4. _____	4. _____
5. _____	5. _____
6. _____	6. _____
7. _____	7. _____
8. _____	8. _____
9. _____	9. _____
10. _____	10. _____

trusted adviser, as well as copies of the content and style checklists, to help guide the person in giving you the critique.

This step is useful because we can't always see everything about our own presentations. For example, you may be listening to content so closely that you miss some relevant concerns about your style. Or, you may be so focused on how you're using your hands that you stop listening to how well you make your points.

In selecting a trusted adviser, be sure to ask someone who really cares about you and wants you to succeed. Make sure that person also speaks well, or at least understands the basics of good speaking. Ask the person to be candid and constructive about your performance. Give the person permission to provide you with all of the feedback. Even trusted advisers will not be comfortable giving you suggestions unless you explicitly give them permission.

Step 4: Complete the Personal Assessment Questionnaire

The next step is to fill out the Personal Assessment Questionnaire on page 73. This questionnaire is designed to look at all of the aspects of your communication style. You may answer the questions by typing them out on your computer or just taking out a legal pad and jotting down the answers. Either way, I recommend that you write down the answers so you can refer back to them later. Write as much or as little as you like. Set aside enough time to be thorough; this can be an interesting process of self-discovery.

Step 5: Interview Trusted Advisers

You have already identified a trusted adviser or two to review your videotape. You may ask the same person, or some other people, to fill out the Trusted Adviser Survey on pages 74 and 75 to provide outside perspective on your skills. Once again, anyone you involve in this process should

■ **Personal Assessment Questionnaire**

1. What are my strengths in communication?
2. What do others tell me they like about my communication style?
3. When am I most comfortable talking to other people?
4. Who are my best "audiences"?
5. What are my weaknesses as a communicator?
6. Presentation skills evaluation—pros and cons.
7. Keynote speeches—pros and cons.
8. Conversation skills—pros and cons.
9. Skill at leading meetings—pros and cons.
10. Listening skills—pros and cons.
11. What have I always avoided doing regarding communication?
12. What are the consequences of my avoidance?
13. What conditions in my professional life have kept me from addressing these issues?
14. What would it actually take to improve?
15. What would be the benefits of improving?
16. What kind of commitment am I willing to make for this process?
17. What are the outcomes I expect?
18. How will I know I have succeeded?

genuinely care about you and want you to succeed. Advisers should also be people who have an opportunity to see you regularly in a business setting so that they can provide you with valuable feedback.

Who are the best people to help you? Sometimes they are family members or close friends. Sometimes they are colleagues you trust. Sometimes they are professionals who are good presenters. You may want advisers who have mastered the areas you want to develop. You don't have to choose someone in your immediate circle.

If you have never asked for feedback, don't worry—it's a great experience. Most people go out of their way to point out your strengths. It is empowering to hear about your strengths from other people. I guarantee that you will find out things you did not know about yourself.

Once again, as these trusted advisers fill out the survey, you should give them explicit advice to be candid and constructive. Some people may be reluctant to critique you unless you tell them it's OK.

■ **Trusted Adviser Survey**

Dear Friend,

This questionnaire is a tool that I am using to build communication skills. I value your opinion and hope that you will provide me with candid, constructive feedback on my strengths and needs. Please write brief answers to the questions below. There is also a space at the bottom of the survey for general comments.

1. What do you see as my strengths in communicating?
2. Can you give me a specific example?
3. What areas of communication need further development?
4. Please give me a specific example.
5. What is the consequence of not developing this area?
6. How do you believe other people react to this?
7. What would be the best way for me to address this need?
8. What other areas of communication could I work on?
9. Why are those important?
10. Please rate my skills in these specific areas:
    - Presentations
    - Speeches
    - Leading meetings
    - Conversation
    - Listening
    - Writing

11. Please tell me how I do with these groups:
    - Direct reports
    - Colleagues
    - Board of directors
    - Customers
    - Industry analysts
    - Reporters and editors
    - Other important constituencies
12. Assess my executive presence such as:
    - Posture and body language
    - Wardrobe and style
    - Personal grooming
    - Office decor and environment
13. What else do I need to know in order to grow?
14. Are there any other comments you have that would contribute to my work?

Step 6: Create Your Personal Balance Sheet

Now it's time to use all the information you have gathered to fill out the Personal Balance Sheet on page 76. Review your Videotape Work Sheets, your Personal Assessment Questionnaire, and the Trusted Adviser Surveys. Be sure to note patterns or comments you see more than once. If

▪ Personal Balance Sheet

Strengths	Needs
1. _____	1. _____
2. _____	2. _____
3. _____	3. _____
4. _____	4. _____
5. _____	5. _____
6. _____	6. _____
7. _____	7. _____
8. _____	8. _____
9. _____	9. _____
10. _____	10. _____

comments are frequently repeated, they need to be recorded in your strengths or weakness column. You will likely see some outliers—comments that seem off-the-wall. If they are not repeated, they probably are just one person's opinion. You may want to take a few days to reflect on all the information before you fill out your Personal Balance Sheet.

Taking stock of your skills will help you see the big picture: your assets and your liabilities. This invaluable process opens your eyes as to where your communication skills stand and allows you to create a vision of where you'd like them to be. Once you have a complete assessment of your skills, you can create a plan to get farther, faster. Businesses have plans, and so should you.

8

Creating a Plan: Leaders Know It's the Way to Get Farther, Faster

*"I'm a great believer in luck, and I find
the harder I work, the more I have of it."*

—Thomas Jefferson, 3rd U.S. President

CREATING A PLAN HELPS ensure that you set things in motion. By writing out a plan of action, you are able to see what it is you would like to accomplish—and how to get there. Think of it as writing out a grocery list. Without a list, you remember some items you need while you're at the store but often find you've forgotten a handful once you're home. However, by taking a few minutes to sit down and write out what groceries you need, you'll be sure to get everything on your list. Your coaching plan will function the same way.

Failing to Plan

Without a plan, "someday" never comes. A partner in an accounting firm was busy with demanding clients and a heavy travel schedule. He considered getting a speaking coach but decided it just didn't fit it into his schedule. One year passed. The firm asked him to give a keynote speech at an international conference. He had a few weeks to prepare; that's when I got a call.

We had trouble finding time on his calendar, but a week before the event, he booked a session. Forty minutes before the session, a client emergency forced him to cancel. When he finally came in, he still had not even reviewed the PowerPoint slides for his presentation. He had also been up until 3:00 in the morning on a call with a difficult client. So again, he went home, and he came back with only one day to work on the presentation. We did our best. But the last thing he said before he left for the conference was, "I wish I had come in earlier."

Failing to plan is planning to fail. The best you can expect is to get through it. Creating a plan helps you set aside the time you need to work on your skills.

Creating the Plan

You should create your personal coaching plan around your needs and your calendar. This is essential to your success. You probably can't take a sabbatical to work on communication skills. You must fit it in with the rest of your activities.

The personal coaching plan is like a fitness program: you put in time each week and you lose a few pounds. The results keep you motivated. You give a good speech, and people compliment you. You feel that the investment of time was worth it, and you want to keep going.

Don't Catch the "Overnight" Success Bug

You wouldn't expect to learn to fly a jetliner in three hours. You would attend flight school and put in lots of hours in the cockpit with an instructor before even flying solo in a single-engine plane. Likewise, you shouldn't expect overnight success in public speaking, presentations, media interviews, or any of the other skills you want to learn.

After one speech, you may expect your skills to improve dramatically. Sometimes it doesn't work that way. You will improve with each event, but you don't have to do it all in one month. Some clients come to coaching and want to check off a list of twenty-five items in one session. It's best to focus on priorities. You will check off the list. Set yourself up for *continuous* learning.

> *"The goals you set for yourself and the strategies you choose become your blueprint or plan."*

—CHARLES GIVENS, American Businessman, Author, and Trainer

Take It Step by Step

In project management, you're taught to break down any big task into individual steps. Let's imagine you want to become a competitive club-level tennis player. We're not talking Wimbledon, just playing competitively enough to get into a club tournament. Perhaps you have played tennis, but just for leisure—you can hit the ball over the net and not embarrass yourself. But it would be a lot more fun—and perhaps good for business—if you could really play and compete.

You might start by sitting in the stands at a tennis club or watching a tournament on television, paying a little more attention to what the great players do to win games. You might even start to imagine yourself on the court, so you pick up your racket and try a swing while you watch. You would start to see the difference between what they do and what you do, right now.

Next, you would sign up for a class and ask the tennis pro to help you. The pro would assess your level of play, share with you what he or she thinks you need to learn to become a competitive player, and start with some basic drills. At first, the drills might feel awkward and unnatural because you've never done them before. But over the next few weeks and months, you would practice those drills until muscle memory set in and the movements began to feel natural. You continue to go to class, practice on your own time, and read books and magazines to study what the pros know. Gradually, you would see and feel some improvement.

Eventually feeling more confident, you sign up for your first tournament to test your skills. You might not win the tournament, but you notice that your skills have definitely improved. You enter the same tournament the following year, and you take home a trophy. But the payoff is greater than a trophy. You're playing and winning, in shape, feeling good, and having fun.

Your Personal Development Plan should work the same way. Make a list of individual activities, like a to-do list, the little steps that will help you achieve your goal. Think of it the same way you think of saving for retirement. If you start saving today, invest regularly, and continue to learn about investing you can accumulate what you need. If you wait until you can *afford* to save (or have time to work on your skills), you may never start and probably will fall short of your goals. Setting up regular opportunities to work on your skills is like automatic deposits into your personal development account.

Getting Started on Your Personal Development Plan

To get started on your plan, we need to gather some information. There are several items you need: your Personal Balance Sheet (from Chapter 7), your professional calendar, and several project folders into which you can throw your materials and a checklist of activities.

Review Your Personal Balance Sheet to Become Familiar with Your Goals

Return to the assessment work you did in Chapter 7: the Personal Balance Sheet. Review the strengths and needs that you identified, including your observations and those of trusted advisers. What jumps out? What is a priority? What do you really want to do better? Circle or put a star next to those items.

For example, let's say you had several notes about working on your voice. You noticed it sounded monotone, and a trusted adviser said you needed to sound more passionate about what you're saying. Put that down as number one on the following list: "What I Want to Do Better."

■ **What I Want to Do Better**

1. _____
2. _____
3. _____
4. _____
5. _____
6. _____
7. _____
8. _____
9. _____
10. _____

Review Your Professional Calendar for Events and Speaking Opportunities

Now it's time to look at your professional calendar for the next six months and see what is coming up. What conferences, meetings, and media interviews will you have? Or what would you like to be doing? Board meetings, analyst calls, media interviews, employee roundtables—whatever is there is an opportunity to practice.

One of the keys to creating a successful plan is to build your learning around real-life events. These are the things you would do anyway in the course of your work. Look ahead and identify events far enough in the future for you to do some preparation and practice.

Create a Project Folder for Each Event

Viewing each event as a separate project, create a folder for that project. Inside each folder you will put everything you need, including a to-do list (see page 82) for that project only. You will want to choose the events that are a challenge for you. If employee meetings are easy, but you have more trouble in formal presentations or media interviews, make folders for those and start gathering the materials you need for each.

Make a to-do list for each folder. If you have a speech, you need to research or meet with the speechwriter; put that on your list. If you are working on your voice, you will want to purchase a tape recorder so you can play it back and listen to your inflection and pace; put it on your list to remind yourself. Perhaps you want to add more humor to your speeches. You may jot down "read a book on humor," "visit some humor websites," or "hire a humor writer."

Also in the folder you will include elements for the presentation or items of interest: a story, a newspaper article, copies of the slides, talking points—anything that will help you.

Once you have your folder and to-do list together, go back to your calendar and enter related activities *on your schedule*. You must build in time on your calendar for research, writing, and practicing. You will never find time to write or practice if you don't *schedule* it. *Finding* extra time for these activities is about as common as finding an extra $100 bill in a pair of pants.

Writing the activities into your schedule will be a relief; knowing you have set aside time will reduce your anxiety and help you enjoy the

■ **Project Folder Checklist**

1. _____
2. _____
3. _____
4. _____
5. _____
6. _____
7. _____
8. _____
9. _____
10. _____

process. Ninety-eight percent of the time, people feel anxious or unhappy about speaking because they haven't made time to prepare. Put activities on your calendar and give yourself the gift of knowing that you have plenty of time.

Making Your To-Do Lists

Here is a detailed description of *some* of the activities you may put on your to-do lists.

Research

You need new, interesting, and current information to communicate effectively. Audiences want fresh ideas and cutting-edge thinking. One of the obligations of the speaker is to make the presentation worth their time. Whether speaking to a conference, a reporter, your employees, or the public, you have to be constantly looking for new material that will have an impact on your audience.

Research is an ongoing activity, but you may want to set aside specific time to read or go on the Internet. You might want to interview people before an event. You may assign other people to help you with research, but you will need time to review it.

It's a good idea to keep each event file handy so you can throw in items when you find them. If you see something relevant in a book, make a photocopy and put it in the file. Sources of information include magazines, books (don't forget how-to books), newspapers, websites, movies, brochures, comedy shows, radio programs, and television programs. I encourage people to read, watch, or listen to things they don't normally see or hear to get a fresh perspective and to stay current.

Preparation

Preparation includes organizing, writing, and editing. There is no right or wrong way to do this; just have a system that works for you. Once you have gathered information in your files, you can sort through it and start organizing, outlining, and writing.

Why create an outline? I learned a lot about that from writing this book. An outline helps you see on paper what is there, as well as what is missing. By writing it down, you can study it and get ideas before you begin writing your remarks or putting together slides. One mistake many people make is creating slide presentations from the slides they already have in their computers before they *think about what they want to say* and create an outline.

Depending on the event or project, in the preparation phase, you may want to write down the following items:

- The big idea
- Three main points
- Questions your audience (or the reporter) might have
- A story
- Talking points
- Elements/graphs for slides

Should you write out what you are going to say, jot down bullet points, or make note cards? That depends on two factors: your personal preference and the type of presentation you are giving. A formal keynote is typically written out. A meeting is typically done from an agenda. An informal meeting may work best from note cards.

Practice

You have to practice to give a good presentation. The top speakers in the world practice a presentation several times before they give it. You can cheat on practice time, but as parents all over the world say, "You will only be cheating yourself." Practice not only helps you perform better but also reduces anxiety because you are confident and prepared.

Go into a conference room or close your office door and review the materials while sitting in your chair. Read or scan the notes out loud. Then stand up and go through your presentation in real time. Practice out loud *several* times. I do not recommend practicing out loud in your car, because you will be distracted, or on a plane, because you cannot speak loudly enough (unless you want to annoy your seatmate).

Here are some other tips on practice:

■ **Don't wait until the last minute.** Depending on the length of the talk, you may need a completed script a week or two in advance so you can practice several times. Put it on your calendar as an appointment with yourself.

■ **Use a mirror.** Since you are your own toughest critic, by watching yourself in a mirror, you will be able to recognize distracting gestures, awkward stances, and wandering eye contact right away. Don't use this technique until you have already practiced without the mirror so you know the material reasonably well.

■ **Record audio and/or video.** Play back a recording of your speech. This will help you identify areas that need improvement. With an audio recording, you'll be able to hear annoying vocal habits, areas of hesitation or uncertainty, and awkward sentence structures.

■ **Don't memorize.** If you try to memorize your remarks, you are in too much danger of forgetting what you want to say. Learn concepts, practice phrasing, but don't be a slave to saying it word-for-word the way it's written.

■ **Use a script or an outline.** Practice enough so that the words on your note cards or outline are so familiar that you only have to glance at them. That will make you look prepared and sound more natural.

■ **Time your presentation.** If you must meet a time requirement, timing your presentation will help you decide what to cut or what to expand. One of the cardinal rules of speaking is to never take more time than you've been given.

■ **Use a friendly test audience.** Having a trusted colleague or mentor listen to your presentation will help you begin to get comfortable in front of other people.

■ **Visualize success.** As you practice, learn how to see the audience in your mind's eye. The more you can imagine the room, the people, the smiles, the applause, and yourself at the podium in control, the more successful you will be when the day comes.

What Else Can You Do?

As you check off the items on your project to-do lists, you may want to have resources to help you. You can assemble a team, hire a coach, read books, or enroll in classes. The rest of this chapter has advice on how to find and use those resources.

Assemble Your Team

You may have a team of people inside your organization to support your communications. If you don't, now would be a good time to identify the best people you can get. Arnold Zetcher, president and CEO of Talbots, has Margery Myers, VP of Communications. "She knows how I think, and how I want to say things," Zetcher says.

"We clicked right away," says Myers. "Now after many years, it's like we're attached by Vulcan mind-merger. I can tell how he feels by looking at him. If he puts only a line next to something, I know what he means."

Your team should not only support you but also be in the inner circle. "You have to have someone you trust," says Zetcher. "Margery is in on almost everything I'm doing, as much as anyone in the company. She knows what I want to say. I trust her completely."

In addition to communications professionals, some CEOs regularly talk with senior leaders in their companies to get a "reading" on how they are doing. They can find out what impressions employees have after a meeting, or what clients thought of a presentation.

Hire a Coach

A good coach will help you develop a plan and execute it. You do the work, but you have professional guidance. A professional should meet with you regularly and keep you on course. A professional can also give you feedback that no one else can, and sometimes that is validating. "I had formal coaching, and it helped me gain a degree of confidence that I was going in the right direction," said one CEO. "Hearing that, you can improve much, much faster," he observed.

In addition to speaking coaches, there are speechwriters, humorists, media trainers, and PR people who can help you develop and practice your skills. When searching for a coach, trainer, or speechwriter, you should interview a few different people. They don't necessarily need to know your industry inside out—they need to know their field. Find out about the methods they use, how often you will see them, and who else they have worked with.

You should also have good chemistry with a coach, speechwriter, or trainer. Coaching is a personal endeavor. Share your concerns honestly with candidates and see how they respond. See if they are constructive and still candid. You want support and honesty in equal parts.

Read Books and Articles

I once had a client who said, "I don't have time for all these coaching sessions. Can't you just give me a book so I can read it? That's how I learn." I sent him several books, but I was not sure it was the right thing to do. He told me after reading the books that he had "figured it out," so I taped a presentation. He was still struggling. Books are great, but you still need practical experience.

When looking for books, don't just go to the business section. If you want to learn humor, go to the comedy section; if you want to enhance your wardrobe or image, try searching those words in your favorite online bookstore. Don't forget about CDs; listening to books in your car is a great way to use your time efficiently.

Enroll in Workshops and Classes

I really enjoy attending workshops because they provide opportunities to learn from the experts, and you also have a chance to talk to other people in the class. I belong to the National Speakers Association, which provides outstanding workshops and seminars. The members are experts, consultants, coaches, and humorists who make a living in public speaking. Even though they are professionals, most of them go to learn. Even the most successful say that attending these workshops is one of the keys to their success.

There are many places where you can find communication skills courses, including industry conferences, public seminars, and professional associations. You never know what you might pick up that will make all the difference in your personal development plan.

PART 2

The Situations

A Survival Guide for the Events Where

You Must Speak and Be Great

9

Speeches

*"Don't speak until you're sure you have something
significant to say—and . . . understand it so well
you could explain it to an eight-year-old."*

—MARIO CUOMO, Former Governor of New York

CEOs GIVE SPEECHES. It doesn't mean they like it. Many experienced speakers don't enjoy it. However, giving a *good* speech can make it a lot more fun.

One particular bank vice president often turned down speaking engagements; she was busy and had no time to practice. As a result, she was not a good speaker and hated getting up in front of an audience. But one day, she was invited to speak at a worldwide conference on women in banking—one of her passions. She decided it was finally time to learn to deliver a good speech, and she enlisted my services.

We talked through her themes, came up with some good stories, and practiced together. As the speech came together, she got excited about it because it was far more interesting than other speeches she had given. Her interest in the topic helped motivate her to practice. She developed more confidence; she had better timing, pauses, and inflection; and her face was alive as she spoke. Now she was animated and energized. She gave a good speech that impressed the audience. Soon, she was being asked to speak often, and she accepted. She traveled with the same speech, modifying it for different audiences. We dubbed it her "speech in a drawer," because when someone called and asked her to speak, she could say yes, knowing she had the basic material in hand. Having the good speech helped her develop the polish and confidence to be an effective speaker.

All good speeches start with a message. You need something significant to say—one clear theme. Once you have a theme, outline your topic. It's best to go for a few (usually three) main points. People can't remember more than that. There are different types of speeches—inaugural addresses, acceptance speeches, motivational talks, policy speeches, openings, roasts, eulogies, and many more—but you should always have a clear theme and a few main points.

At the podium, you may be tempted to change the *way* you speak, to sound more like a "speech." Don't do it. Be yourself. Talk to the audience as if you're talking to a friend over a cup of coffee. Be conversational. Short words and sentences are better than long ones. Speak exactly as you do in a conversation. It's the only way to come across as you. Get rid of the jargon. Eliminate the marketing language. Forget the fancy phrases. Say everything simply and directly.

There are several elements that will bring your speech alive and make it interesting. Those elements include the following:

- Stories
- Audience
- Humor
- Analogies
- Startling facts
- Anecdotes
- Current events

Stories: A Great Beginning (and Middle and End)

You must begin well. One of the best ways to start a speech is with a story. The story should introduce a pivotal theme of your speech. It isn't enough to tell just any funny or interesting story—it should be relevant to the main theme. The story can have suspense, conflict, and/or humor, and it should introduce your topic. The story should be something that your audience will understand. You also may want to put yourself into the story, although you should not be the focus.

When you put yourself in the story, as an observer or as a player, people learn something about you. When they learn something about you, they become more interested in you. Whatever your topic, audiences want to know about you; vignettes help them understand where you're coming from and why you are there. One caution: avoid making yourself the central character of the first story. That can come across as arrogant or self-centered. Speaker, author, and storyteller Marcia Reynolds taught me, "In the beginning of your speech, you have not yet *earned the right* to focus on yourself."

Original stories always work best with an audience. Repeating other speakers' stories is risky. Your audience may already have heard them. Audiences want to know your point of view, what you have seen, or how you see the world. Original stories don't have to be about you; they can be about people, places, and events you have witnessed or heard about. *Your* stories are authentic and more interesting. It's worth taking time to come up with original ones.

Finding your own stories isn't as hard as it may sound. Begin keeping a journal, either a notebook or a computer file, of events, challenges, conflicts, surprises, and learning experiences from your everyday life. When something interesting happens, even if it's just the kernel of an idea, jot it down. It may take a few weeks or even months to fully develop the story, but by keeping a journal, you kick your brain into gear.

In my view, a good story has two elements: conflict and a few well-placed details. Conflict carries people along and keeps them in suspense, making them wonder what's going to happen. Detail makes it real; the audience is able to see how it looked or to hear how it sounded. Descriptions of people or places, dates, times, visuals, sounds, nicknames—a few of these go a long way. Don't go overboard with detail; provide just enough to make it real.

Once you have a good story, keep it. The same story can make a lot of different points. You'll want to start a separate journal to keep track of your best stories. Larry Lucchino, CEO of the Boston Red Sox, has a personal journal, *The Brockett Book*, compiled by his mentor Bill Brockett, a colleague from Yale Law School. When Brockett died, Lucchino kept the journal and added his own stories, famous quotes, funny lines, anecdotes, and words of wisdom. *The Brockett Book*—which rivals the New York yellow pages in length—is an amazing resource, and it keeps growing. Lucchino explains, "If I see a newspaper article, I put it in. It's alphabetized so you can find everything from funny lines on economics and law to serious quotes from Emerson and Oscar Wilde."

Talk *About* Your Audience, Not *to* Them

As you write your speech, think about your audience first. What do they want to know? Why are they there? What can you say that will make it worth their while? No speech can succeed without acknowledging the audience. If you don't have an audience, you don't have a speech! The members of the audience have given you their time. You are obligated to make it worth their while.

Not only should you focus on their interests, but also you should talk about your audience. Mention people by name; talk about their organization, business, city, or town; and reveal what you know, appreciate, or understand about them. This is an art. It's more than saying, "It's so nice to be invited to speak to the XYZ Association." Be specific; mention names, real places, funny or interesting observations, and what you know or wonder about them.

Here is a sample of a speech that UPS chairman Mike Eskew gave to employees about why the company was changing its logo:

> *Our brand is all about our people and keeping the UPS promise. Just as Marty Peters . . . . Marty's the longest-tenured active employee at UPS—out of 360,000 around the world. Marty is a fifty-seven-year veteran of UPS. That's right; he started with us in 1946 . . . and guess what . . . he still shows up at the job every day as a shifter and a customer-counter clerk in Detroit.*
> *And there's someone else we've brought to New York for this special day . . . Ron Sowder, a Kentucky District feeder*

driver. Ron's been with the company forty-two years. In fact, he started in 1961 . . . the year of our last logo change. When Ron started with the company . . . he wasn't old enough to drive. But today he carries the distinction of having the most years of safe driving among active employees in the company. In my book, Ron and Marty are UPS heroes. They not only represent the brand . . . like you—they live the brand every day.

In talking *about* the audience, you pay tribute to them. An authentic leader includes the audience as a group or as individuals—or both. People love to hear about themselves, and more important, they love to know that a leader knows them. This is why a leader always looks for ways to cleverly include the audience in every speech.

Use Humor to Make a Point with Just the Right Touch

"Intelligence is measured by a sense of humor."

—ROGER MARINO, Founder, EMC

As I mentioned in Chapter 5, the power of humor in a speech cannot be overestimated. Speakers who use humor instantly connect with the audience. Audiences see a speaker who is funny as more competent, confident, and intelligent. When people laugh, they are ready to listen.

You don't have to be David Letterman to be funny. You just need to dissect humor and try to re-create it in your own way. Self-effacing humor works well. Abraham Lincoln once said, "If I were two-faced, would I be wearing this one?" Humor about disaster or trouble is also powerful. After Ronald Reagan was shot, he turned to his surgeons and said, "I hope you are Republicans."

Do you *have* to include humor in a speech? There's a saying among professional speakers, "You don't have to use humor . . . unless you want to get paid." As a speaker, you don't have to use humor unless you want to be *effective*. Humor makes a point, and it's a lot more fun. It's better for you and for the audience. You don't have to leave them howling. Just try to make people smile.

One political leader I know has used the same opening joke at many events. While some members of his audience have heard the joke several times, it still gets a laugh. Generally, it's not a good idea to use the same joke over and over. It gets tired. But one well-told joke is always better than none at all.

When it comes to creating original humor, remember that it's most effective when it's specific to the audience or the topic. When you come up with something specific, people think you are a genius. So, how do you develop original humor? Comedy writers suggest that you start by noticing what is ridiculous, absurd, or painful—a problem to which your audience can relate. Writers for the late-night television shows kick around the absurdity of the day's events. Sitcom writers come to work and banter about the stuff that happens to them day in and day out. Once they seize on an event with a painful, ridiculous, or absurd angle, they work it over until it's funny.

There are many books on writing and speaking with humor. You can also hire humorists to help you generate funny lines for your speeches. If you want to write some of your own, my advice is just to get started. Pay attention to what people are worrying or complaining about. Audiences appreciate it when you are plugged in and can make what's painful or upsetting seem OK. Once you have identified the pain, give it a twist. Let's take a look at how to create simple, original *smile lines* with two devices I like to use: an opposite and an exaggeration.

Let's say I want to tell my book editor in an e-mail that I'm behind in finishing the last few chapters of a manuscript. I could say: "I know I am behind, so I'm going to bring my laptop on vacation so I can write the next two chapters, even though my family will be unhappy." Or, I could use an *opposite* and give it a lighter touch: "I'm taking my laptop—that should make me very *popular* with the family." Or, I could exaggerate: "I've rewritten Chapter 16 about thirty-five times—maybe the ocean air will get oxygen into my brain." I am not a comedy writer, and that isn't hilarious, but it's another way to say the same thing with a little lighter touch.

"Tragedy is when I cut my finger. Comedy is when you walk into an open sewer and die."

—MEL BROOKS, Comedian

One of the funniest speeches I have ever heard was delivered by Teri Garr, a wonderful actor and comedian who was diagnosed with multiple sclerosis. Within a few short years, she was severely affected by the disease. The night of the speech, she walked slowly to the podium with a cane and struggled physically with fatigue. But her speech was brilliant. She used humor to explain the challenges and trials of living with MS. Teri Garr's brilliant speech helped her audience really absorb the message. It broke down barriers between those who have MS and those who don't and helped every person in that room embrace the cause.

Start looking at challenges, difficulties, and pain through a different lens and you will be able to use humor effectively. Humor is everywhere. You simply have to notice it.

Use Analogies to Help People Understand

Whatever concept you want to explain, it's always easier with a good analogy. Analogies are economical devices for instantly capturing a concept. They are similarities, equivalents, parallels, or opposites that help people grasp and remember an idea. For example: "The Internet is like an information superhighway." "A boycott is voting with your wallet." Analogies define a concept or explain how it works.

Analogies can make a speech. Jane Tisdale, head of Global Structured Products for State Street Global Advisors, spoke to stockbrokers on the virtues of quantitative investing—a somewhat foreign topic even to investment professionals. The quantitative approach uses computer models to sift through huge amounts of data and find well-performing, overlooked but underpriced stocks.

Jane and her team needed to explain the process and convince the audience that computerized number crunching works. They decided to write the whole speech as a baseball analogy, using *Moneyball*, by Michael Lewis, as a point of reference. *Moneyball* tells the story of how Billy Beane, the Oakland A's general manager, used readily available but widely overlooked statistics to exploit inefficiencies in hiring players. This helped him assemble a group of players with one of the lowest payrolls that won more regular-season games than any other team except the Seattle Mariners.

Here's an excerpt from the speech:

> *Major-league scouts follow the traditional approach of traveling from town to town to watch high school and college baseball games and identify the next Pedro Martinez . . . in their search for greatness they may focus on the pitcher with style or the "Sammy Sosa–like" batter who hits the big home runs. The alternative is to take the Billy Beane statistical approach to broaden their scope and uncover hidden gems from the ranks of Triple A clubs or the low end of the draft.*

When searching for analogies, you can look in books—but don't stop there. Anything you can see, feel, picture, or imagine can be used in an analogy. The analogy should be to something that your hearers already know or understand. Once you start looking, you'll find them. Analogies are often the most memorable of all messages.

Use Startling Facts to Punch It Up

Startling facts are good because they add the element of surprise. Startling facts are also convincing. When you surprise an audience with something they didn't know, they are prepared to hear the rest of what you have to say.

Startling facts are everywhere. Information is all around you. Pick up the *Wall Street Journal*, your local newspaper, or any magazine on any given day and you'll find them. Collect them and throw them into file folders. Go on the Internet and use a search site; in an instant, you can now find what used to take hours to retrieve in a library. Startling facts can also be a great way to start a presentation. The fresher they are, the more you impress your audience with your current research and thinking.

Use Anecdotes to Make Memorable Points

Anecdotes are different from stories; they are usually short narratives of an interesting, amusing, or biographical incident. They are not necessarily funny. Anecdotes capture the essence of a person, place, or situation. Former British prime minister Margaret Thatcher, an eloquent speaker, is brilliant at this. In her eulogy for President Reagan, she weaved a vignette of his life using one-line anecdotes:

> *Ronnie himself certainly believed that he had been given back his life for a purpose. As he told a priest after his recovery, "Whatever time I've got left now belongs to the Big Fella Upstairs."*
>
> *When his aides were preparing option papers for his decision, they were able to cut out entire drafts of proposals that they knew "the Old Man" would never wear.*

The secret to a good anecdote is to capture what's extraordinary, interesting, or funny in just a few words. When looking for anecdotes, consider stories you know or have heard about a person or situation, and boil them down to the nugget. Give the audience credit: you don't have to tell all of a story to make your point. Distill it until you encapsulate the idea. In the hands of a good speaker, an anecdote is like pure gold.

Use Current Events to Relate Your Ideas

A quote or moment from a current movie, book, song, or TV show can also be a great way to communicate a message. I recently came across a speech that Lou Holtz, the legendary University of Notre Dame football coach, used to give to his incoming freshmen every year. The speech uses the device of quoting from a comic strip to introduce Holtz's brand of shaping up the team:

> Gentlemen, in the comic strip "Pogo," there was a character who once said, "The solution is obvious, wither we become them or they become us." I can assure everyone in this room that we are not going to become you. You must become Notre Dame. I want you to learn everything we do at Notre Dame, how we do it, why we do it. It's important that you learn our methods now so that when you become juniors or seniors you can provide the proper leadership for our younger players. That is essential if we are to enjoy success. We did not recruit you to change the University of Notre Dame but to conform to the morals and values of this great institution. You won't change Notre Dame, but Notre Dame is going to change you.

"Pogo" wouldn't be relevant today; it was current in Lou Holtz's coaching days. But you can find your own sources by opening the newspaper, watching a movie, or reading a book. Citing TV's hot new show, celebrity, sporting event, or happening that has captured attention can be a great way to relate your ideas. Current events make your presentation seem new and up-to-date.

Bring Facts and Figures to Life

> *"The main part of intellectual education is not the acquisition of facts but learning how to make facts live."*
>
> —Oliver Wendell Holmes, American Judge

Facts and figures can be powerful, but they can also be a bore. When you use them, use them appropriately and judiciously. Make them live. Incorporate within your facts and figures what's really interesting: people and examples that bring the facts alive.

I worked with former Massachusetts governor Jane Swift on her State of Education speech in 2002. Massachusetts had recently passed a law making a statewide comprehensive exam mandatory in the public schools.

The first version of Governor Swift's speech highlighted how many students were passing the Massachusetts Comprehensive Assessment System (MCAS) test:

> *I'm pleased to announce today that even more students are sharing your success. Following the May retest, nearly 85 percent of the class of 2003 has passed the math portion of the MCAS.*

It may seem apparent to you that there is a problem with that statement: more than 15 percent of students were failing. This would be unacceptable to critics. Here's how we highlighted the positive side of the statistic by bringing people into it:

> *These numbers are very encouraging, but what inspires me most are the stories of success—students like Thomas Martin, from Durphy High, in Fall River, who is here with us today.*
>
> *Like many juniors his age, Tom dealt with the pressure of balancing both school and work. But unlike many students, he also dealt with the overwhelming pain of losing his father, grandparents, and uncle—all within a short period of time. School was the last thing on his mind, and his first MCAS scores showed it.*
>
> *But Tom refused to give up. He attended every in-school and after-school extra-help program at Durphy. He sought guidance and advice from his teachers—and support from his mom. And last December, Tom didn't just succeed in passing MCAS; he excelled—jumping twenty-eight points in English and twelve in math. I want to congratulate Tom for his success and his determination.*

Numbers don't always make your case, and they can be dull, dull, dull. Make your case by using people, places, and events that bring the numbers alive.

Speaking Style

Once you have put these elements into your speech, it's time to focus on presentation style. As you practice, keep the tips in this section in mind to help you develop a strong presence and *own* the platform.

Tip 1: Find Your Authentic Personal Style of Expression

When giving a speech, you should not worry about impressing people with polish. However, you should have enough polish to convey your message with ease. A CEO must own the platform. You don't own it by simply walking on stage with confidence. You own the platform when you look completely comfortable up there. Your posture, voice, facial expression, movement, gestures, pacing, pauses, and timing all contribute to that comfortable on-stage presence. It's important to master these aspects because audiences connect your ability to *speak* with your ability to *lead*.

Much of the comfort you develop on the platform comes with experience. The more you do something, the more comfortable you are. Comfort also comes from knowing your material. You need to practice every speech until you have internalized the messages.

In developing a speaking style, remember that what's most important is to be true to *you*. Your language, voice, phrasing, accent, and general style expression must be authentic. Many people go into "presentation mode" and speak differently or look different when they get up to the podium. Don't fall into that trap. Instead, use the remaining tips in this section as a guide to create your own comfortable, authentic speaking style.

Tip 2: Body Language

Before you open your mouth to speak, people have already sized you up. The way you stand and move creates a powerful impression. Good speakers appear in control. They know how to move their bodies. Too much movement, such as pacing or waving your hands, makes you appear nervous. Every movement on stage should have a purpose.

Your starting position should be with your legs hip-distance apart, standing tall, and your arms at your sides. Don't cross your arms, put them behind your back, or link your hands together. It may feel natural, but it makes you look nervous. Later, we'll talk about how to use your hands.

Now shift your weight from side to side so you don't seem too stiff. If you want to move to another part of the stage, move deliberately and stay there: don't pace or sway. If you're not sure you appear natural doing this, videotape yourself walking and standing on stage. While it may not feel natural to put your arms at your sides and move purposefully, it will once you have practiced. Videotape one of your speeches. If you see awkward or repetitive movements that could be distracting, stop. Nothing undermines your presence on stage faster than habitual, unnecessary movement.

Tip 3: Facial Expressions

You want to let people know that you are glad to be there: that means smiling and engaging the audience with your eyes. A pleasant smile and steady, focused eye contact conveys volumes about your comfort level. This is how you connect. If you have videotaped a speech, you can look at it again to see how well you are using facial expression to convey emotion.

As you look at the audience, really see them and make a connection. You can do this most of the time unless there are lights in your eyes. Lock in on one group at a time; don't sweep the room from side to side, and instead try to pick out people in the audience and meet their gaze. Even if you're looking at only one person, all the people in that general area will think you are looking at them.

Tip 4: Gestures

Gestures should be short, on point, and descriptive. Use your hands to "draw" a picture. Hands should be at your sides except when you want to illustrate a point. Stand in front of a mirror and try to connect your words with your hands. How would you demonstrate a time line such as "before, then, after"? How would you use your hands to describe "top to bottom"?

How would you show a "broad array of options"? What about counting "first, second, third"?

Once you master a few of these gestures, practice your entire speech in front of a mirror. You don't need to gesture on every sentence, just where it adds to what you are saying.

Tip 5: Voice

The secret to developing a great speaking voice is to be conversational. Too many speakers go flat or monotone when they step to the microphone. Your speaking voice should have the same qualities as your conversational voice—volume, pitch, inflection, tone, pace, accent, and phrasing. If you don't know whether you sound conversational, you should make a tape of your voice during a speech.

Common problems include the following:

- A monotone voice that sounds as if you're reading
- Pacing that is too fast or too slow
- Awkward phrasing or word choices
- Pronunciations that are unusual or formal
- Volume that is too loud or too soft

"Talk low, talk slow, and don't say too much."

—John Wayne, Actor

To develop a conversational style, you have to know your speech well. If you know what you're going to say, you will sound as if you're speaking, not reading. Your voice is one of the most powerful assets that you have as a speaker, and it is important to connect with people by being conversational.

Tip 6: Phrasing

Phrase for meaning. Don't articulate each word with the same emphasis. If you pause in the wrong place, you sound stilted and unnatural. Mark your script and practice phrasing until it sounds conversational and natural. For example, you probably know the song lyric "Over the river and through the woods, to Grandmother's house we go."

You wouldn't say: "Over . . . the river . . . and . . . through the . . . woods." Yet, often when you hear speakers who haven't rehearsed or don't know what's coming, they pause in the wrong places.

Learn your script until it sounds conversational: "Over-the-river . . . and . . . through-the-woods . . . to-Grandmother's-house . . . we-go." Phrasing correctly makes you come across as natural.

Tip 7: Appearance

Leaders look crisp and professional all the time, especially on stage. You should dress well for a public speaking engagement. Even if it is business-casual, make sure your clothes fit you, flatter you, and project the image you want to have.

Express your individual style through color and accessories. It's good for a CEO to have a signature look. There are many books on dressing professionally. The rules for professional dress boil down to high quality, great fit, comfortable, and appropriate.

When giving a speech, you should almost always dress in a suit, whether you are a man or a woman. As CEO, you will have occasions to speak in casual settings where business-casual is perfectly fine. The rules for business-casual are the same: nice clothing, just slightly more casual. You still must have quality, fit, comfort, and appropriateness.

Tip 8: Memorizing

I do not advise anyone to memorize a speech from beginning to end. It's practically impossible, and it's unnecessary. However, you should not read your speeches either. You should be extremely familiar with the script so you use it just as a reference.

Once, as a television news reporter, reporting from the field, I blanked out at the end of the lead story. I had memorized my taglines, but my mind went blank—in front of tens of thousands of viewers. Later, back in the newsroom around midnight, producer Paul Gluck sat me down. "What happened?" he asked. "I don't know," I told him. "I memorized it—thought I knew it. I had gone over it many times!" Paul observed, "That was your first mistake. Memorizing doesn't work. If you forget a single word, you forget everything that follows." Remember concepts and phrases, but don't memorize word-for-word.

Tip 9: Teleprompter

Teleprompters, the devices that scroll the copy in front of the television lens or in front of a speaker during a speech, are great inventions. The teleprompter dramatically improves eye contact. But you have to know how to use it, or you'll look as if you're reading, thereby defeating the purpose.

Even if you have a teleprompter, you should practice your speech at least five or six times so you don't have to rely on the prompter. Your goal is to learn and *internalize* the messages. Once you really know your speech, the prompter will just prompt, or remind you what to say. And don't let your eyes move from side to side: look straight ahead. Darting eyes are a dead giveaway that you are reading.

Summary

- **Last-minute tip:** Right before you deliver a speech, practice the beginning and end out loud. This will help ensure that you start well and finish with a bang.

- **If you have more time:** Record your entire speech on an audio-cassette, and play it back. Listen carefully to check your timing and delivery of stories, anecdotes, and humor. Make improvements.

- **Plan for ongoing improvement:** Keep a journal of stories, humor, and material that you can use in speeches. Many stories can be used in a variety of speeches to make the same point. Make time to write out your stories; it's easier to edit and improve them when you are able to see them in black-and-white.

10

Presentations

"A good presentation will earn you a company-wide
reputation as an expert in your job."

—Jeffrey J. Fox, Author, *How to Become CEO*

Webster's defines a *presentation* as "something offered or given, a descriptive or persuasive account, for the attention of the mind." When you think of a presentation as a gift, it takes on a new meaning. As a presenter, you should offer a *gift for the mind*.

In this discussion, I'm defining a presentation as different from a speech. I think of a presentation as a "working speech." It's a practical, content-driven, specific, detailed treatment of a topic. A presentation focuses on informing. The information helps the audience. It educates, provokes discussion, creates debate, enhances decisions, or sells a product or service. Very often a presentation includes visual materials such as slides, charts, blueprints, presentation books, work sheets, brochures, and samples, as well as demonstrations, role play, music, or some type of audience experience.

As CEO, you might give a presentation to your board, investors, the executive team, employees, customers, industry analysts, or the media. You have many audiences and give many types of presentations. That's why you need to develop this most basic skill.

Presentations are similar to speeches in some ways. As with a speech, the focus of a presentation must be your audience. Sometimes you don't know much about your audience. You need to know so you can create a presentation that interests them. That's why I developed the following Audience Agenda System—a technique for presenters to create audience-focused presentations.

■ Audience Agenda System

There are four steps to the Audience Agenda System.

Step 1: Write down your topic and describe your audience.
Topic and Audience

_____

_____

_____

Step 2: Write down your agenda for your presentation.
Write out everything you want to do in this meeting: what you want people to know, information they should have, what you hope to persuade them to do, what action you would like them to take.
My Agenda

_____

_____

_____

Step 3: Now write down your audience agenda.
Forget about what *you* want. Imagine you are actually sitting in the chairs along with the members of your audience. Why are they there? What is keeping them awake at night? What are their problems and needs? What questions do they want you to answer? Why have they given up their valu-

able time to listen to your presentation? Even if you don't *know* your audience members, you should know why they are there, or find out. Once you have that knowledge, write down the audience agenda.

Audience Agenda

_____

_____

_____

_____

Step 4: Compare these two agendas side by side.

If you have done the exercise properly—really thinking the way your audience does—you will probably find that the two agendas are different. There may be some similarities, but most people find that their own agenda is different from their audience's agenda.

Usually I ask clients to *throw out their agenda* and work strictly from the audience agenda. That's right—you already know *your* agenda. It's time to focus on the audience. Show them you know them. Write down the agenda for your presentation based on why your audience is there.

Presentation Agenda

_____

_____

_____

_____

_____

_____

_____

This system has helped hundreds of clients like you take a strategic approach to audience interests. I developed this system because while many presentation books tell you that you should focus on the audience, some presenters find the advice difficult to put into practice. Some say they don't know much about a particular audience and have little opportunity to find out. This method will help you overcome that information gap.

The Audience Agenda System aids you in thinking through your own agenda versus the *audience's* agenda. When you do this exercise, you'll find that you know more than you imagined. Even if you have never met or spoken to anyone in your audience, this system works. Do the exercise and you will be able to generate, organize, and present relevant material.

The beauty of this unique Audience Agenda System is that it works for *all* of your meetings, whether you know your audience or not. It ensures that you're presenting material that is important to *them*. It takes only a few minutes to do this exercise, and the time is well worth it. You will avoid wasting hours creating presentations that miss the mark with your audience.

If you have ever struggled to decide what to put in and what to leave out, this system will help you. I recommend you do this exercise before you assemble any book, slide show, or handout. Get your agenda in line with the audience, and then create your materials. And put the most important items at the top; that way, if your time is cut short, you will still have covered the parts that are most important to your audience.

"He that speaks much is much mistaken."

—BENJAMIN FRANKLIN, Scientist and Diplomat

No Time to Prepare

A busy marketing executive typically waited until the night before her board presentations to prepare. She would spend hours typing up a report that she would read the next day. The presentations were dull and lifeless. She gave the impression that she didn't know her stuff, even though she did. We needed to come up with a more efficient way for her to prepare these presentations. She told me she would like to get ready for these frequent meetings with thirty minutes to an hour of prep time. So, we developed the Quick Prep Method for organizing any presentation.

Quick Prep Method for Organizing Any Presentation

You start by writing down the questions you know your audience would have if you had to speak on the spot about your topic. Imagine you walked into the meeting and you were told then and there that the group had some questions on the topic. What would they ask? Put yourself in their shoes, and write down a logical sequence of questions that you would hear. The list of questions might look something like this:

Quick Prep Questions
- What is this project or activity?
- Why are we doing it or considering it?
- What are the advantages?
- What are the disadvantages?
- What's it going to cost?
- How did you come up with your recommendation?
- What makes you think it will work?
- What alternatives are there?
- What does this group need to decide?
- How will we measure success?
- What's the next step?

Write down your questions with some space below each, and then jot down the answers in that space. Write in short form, with bullet points or key words. You primarily need the facts and key words at your fingertips. When you are finished writing, you have an outline for your presentation. Each question and answer is a paragraph for your presentation.

To begin each paragraph, you can ask the question, or make a statement. For example, you might say: "Let me share how we came up with this recommendation," or "What's the next step?" If you have listed appropriate questions in a logical order, you have prepared a presentation. And you know it will work because those are the questions your audience would have asked anyway.

The marketing executive revised her haphazard, time-wasting approach to preparing presentations, and it made an immediate impact. She gave far better presentations and actually started looking forward to monthly board meetings. By focusing on the audience, asking the questions and answering them, you make efficient use of your time and make your presentations better.

To PowerPoint or Not to PowerPoint, That Is the Question

Dolores Mitchell, Massachusetts's commissioner of insurance, is a frequent public speaker who *never* uses PowerPoint. She tells organizations that ask her to speak that if they want slides, they should call somebody else. "Go to any presentation and look at the speaker and the screen with PowerPoint," she said. "One hundred percent of the audience will be focused on the screen. This is counterproductive."

Slides are a blessing and a curse for any presentation. Audiences have seen many presentations that use slides, so they are no longer "wowed" by them unless the slides are well designed and implemented. On the other hand, visuals such as slides are an efficient, effective way to convey detailed information. You just don't want the slides to become the focus. The speaker should always be front and center. If you rely too much on slides, you will lose the audience. Slides should just enhance what you say.

Slides should not have too much detail. They should be clean and legible, with large type and colorful graphics. The point of the slide should be easy to grasp. If your print is too small or your slides too detailed, the audience will either listen to you and ignore the slide, or read the slide and ignore you. I have never met anyone who can read and listen at the same time. If you need to provide detail, put it into the addendum of your presentation, not on the slides. You may want to hire a professional graphic designer to help you.

Remember that you and your message are the focus of the presentation. Even when you have detailed information to present, you can bring a presentation alive with stories, examples, questions, startling facts, and all of the other elements we discussed for speeches in Chapter 9.

You may not want to use slides throughout the presentation. If so, turn off the projector or make the screen go black so that the audiences will focus on you again. Managing the technology is as important as creating good slides.

Expert PowerPoint Q&A

For more ideas, graphic designer Ellen Mosner offers a few pointers:

Q: What are the most common mistakes people make when putting together PowerPoint presentations?

A: Too many words—way too many words.

Q: What makes a PowerPoint presentation work?

A: A few bulleted words intended to enhance the speaker's speech—but not mimic it—and of course, pictures and graphics.

Q: How many words should you have on the screen? How many slides per minute or per thirty minutes?

A: I try to encourage the six-by-six rule: six bullets per screen, max; six words per bullet, max.

Q: What are some other tips for making a graphic presentation "audience-friendly"?

A: I think the most important thing would be to *know your audience*. Some groups work well with lots of clip art. Perhaps some of it should be animated. Another presentation might do better with photos, rather than clip art. A "dry" type of audience would probably not want art and might prefer charts to visually show a trend or other message.

Q: What do you wish everybody knew about using graphic presentations?

A: I wish everybody understood that when you're speaking, if your audience is busy reading, they're not hearing you as well as you'd like them to. Nor are they grasping what they're reading, because you're talking. Both listening and reading are compromised.

"Our public men are speaking every day on something, but they ain't saying anything."

—Will Rogers, American Humorist

Presentation Tips

Now that you have analyzed the audience, prepared the visuals, and practiced your presentation, you are ready to deliver. The rest of this chapter provides tips on delivering great presentations so that you make the most of every opportunity.

Be Aware of How You Say It

What you say is important, and so is how you say it. You can deliver the same message many different ways. To be effective, you have to choose your words carefully. Phil Lussier, president of Institutional Division, Citistreet, a division of State Street Bank and Citigroup, tells the story of flying to Cleveland on a business trip. The flight was headed from Cleveland to Salt Lake City.

"The flight attendant came on the public address system and announced that passengers going on to Salt Lake would have to *get off the plane* in Cleveland, because *this* crew was not going on to Salt Lake City. *Twice* she repeated that *this* crew was not their crew," he recalled. "It was really off-putting. Their choice of words made me wonder why the airlines don't *script* for these situations," he said. "If they had just said, 'Ladies and gentlemen, we need to service the plane for your comfort. We would appreciate it if you would exit the plane when we stop in Cleveland,' people would have appreciated it instead of being annoyed."

How does this translate in giving presentations?

"I think it's that *how you say it* matters," said Phil. "I tell people in our organization that it's not what they *think* they say to someone; it's what that person *hears*," said Phil.

Make It Enjoyable: Use Humor Throughout the Presentation

In Chapters 5 and 9, we talked about what is funny—and how to create original humor. Remember, anything that is painful, difficult, challenging, troubling, or anxiety-provoking has potential to be humorous. Don't stop the humor after your opening funny remarks. Sprinkle a little humor throughout your presentation and it will be more enjoyable for you and the audience. As one CEO told me, "The biggest mistake CEOs make in front of audiences is opening with a joke and assuming that's enough— going on with an hour of dribble. That's so dull."

He discovered the secret to keeping his audience involved. "Figure out what makes an audience laugh," he said. "If you find that, you can unlock that audience."

If you are searching to find what will be funny, remember your audience. Go back to your Audience Agenda System and figure out what, in their experience, might be painful or challenging. With good judgment, you can appropriately turn these difficulties into opportunities for a smile, or even a laugh.

Use Inclusive Language

Inclusive language helps you break down the barriers between you and the audience. Words such as *you*, *your*, *our*, and *us* help you connect and make people feel that you're all on the same team. For example, in opening your presentation, you can say, "What I would like to talk to you about . . . ," or better, start with the word *you*: "You have been gracious to invite me to speak to you about . . . " The second approach shows the audience that you are thinking about them from the start.

Inclusive language makes a powerful impression. Recently I worked with an experienced speaker who had not yet mastered inclusive language. During the practice, she opened by saying, "Good afternoon, I'm glad to be here to talk to you about the benefits of our investment product. This is a great product with many benefits, and we have done very well with it."

No, no, no!

How did we turn it around?

"Thank you for the opportunity to meet with you. We appreciate your sharing so much about your organization with us. You provided us with an opportunity to understand many of the issues you face. You have asked us to prepare some thoughts on solutions to those issues. Our agenda focuses on a few of the options you may consider."

What a difference! And they did win the business.

Once you begin using inclusive language regularly, you will naturally move into it. To practice, record your presentation and play it back. Count the number of inclusive words you use. Inclusive language is a subtle, but powerful, technique for winning over any audience. Once you get into the habit, it becomes second nature.

Be a Little Unpredictable

Ann Murphy, vice president for O'Neill Associates, a communications and government relations firm, has helped many CEOs and political leaders prepare speeches and media interviews. After all these years, she says her boss, Tom O'Neill, is still one of the best she's ever seen.

"He will roam the room and ask someone where they grew up, or why they are there today. Pretty soon, people in the room are really engaged, because they think Tom might ask them a question," she said. "Part of it is his Irish wit—he tells a great story. But it's also because he's unpredictable. People don't know what's going to happen next. They are waiting to be asked a question. This makes him a very engaging speaker."

How does O'Neill find the time to come up with different stories and anecdotes for each presentation? Ann says the staff tracks him down before presentations to debrief him on the audiences to which he's speaking. They do this well in advance—a week or two before the presentation—to allow him time to think about what he can do to add a little fun to his presentation. That way, he has time to tailor jokes and anecdotes for his speech that'll help him draw in the audience.

To be unpredictable, you need time to play with concepts. Consider what you might do that would be a little different or out of the ordinary. You also need to watch other good speakers for effective tools. There is nothing wrong with borrowing something that works, like walking around and asking questions of the audience. Just do it your way. Audiences love it when you shake things up and make it memorable.

Words Matter

If you control the language, you can control the conversation. Words matter. In the mid-1990s, car dealers were looking for ways to sell millions of leased cars that were returned to their lots. The term "reconditioned used cars" was not very appealing. Luxury nameplates like Mercedes-Benz and Lexus created a better term: "certified, preowned vehicles."

Consumers got a good deal on a two- to three-year-old car that came with a warranty and the manufacturer's seal of approval. Sales boomed. The number of cars sold jumped from 452,829 in 1997 to 1,160,707 in 2002, according to CNW Marketing Research, Inc. Now nearly all brands of cars offer such a program. Simply changing the language eliminated one of the major drawbacks to buying a used car and drew customers to the dealerships.

Choosing your words wisely can sell an idea. You can manage the outcome if you manage your words. Language should be accurate, descriptive, and clear. Spend time thinking about word choices and phrases.

Invent Catchy Phrases to Help Them Remember

I am not a big fan of slogans and taglines; they can be fodder for mockery at the water cooler. However, a really catchy phrase can be effective in expressing a concept or value—that is *if* it's catchy, relevant, and not over-the-top.

For example, vacationing in Bermuda one summer, my family got into the taxi at the airport and were reminded instantly why we didn't want to rent mopeds. In Bermuda, they drive on the left side of the road. As we zipped along the winding, two-lane road with hedges walling both sides of the thoroughfare, we wondered why we didn't see more accidents.

I asked the taxi driver, "How do Americans remember to drive on the left?"

"Sometimes they don't!" he said, laughing. "But we have a simple rule," he explained. "Left is right, and right is wrong." Now, there's an easy-to-remember slogan that's relevant and clever but not over-the-top.

If you want your audience to remember something, you can make it easier with a catchy phrase. Don't make it *too* cute. But if something comes to you, try it out on someone, and use it if it works. It may be the perfect way to make a point stick.

The Picture Can Be the Message

Dr. JoAnn Manson, chief of the Division of Preventive Medicine and codirector of the Center for Women's Health at Brigham and Women's Hospital, Harvard Medical School, gave a presentation to a group of high-level businesswomen. I have to admit, I wondered how she would get them interested so early in the morning on what my husband has cleverly dubbed a *homework topic*: "Women's Health: Taking the Initiative." Homework is something you have to see or hear; it's important, but you don't necessarily have to like it.

As JoAnn stepped to the podium, you could feel the audience girding themselves for a lecture on heart disease and obesity. But she won them over right from the start with a great visual: a photo of an escalator next to a flight of stairs in a crowded shopping mall. On the staircase, a lone woman was ascending; on the escalator, at least a dozen men and women stood passively as they rode up, expending precious few calories. The audience burst into laughter. The speaker paused, smiled, and said little—no lecture was needed. We got it.

Visuals can be the most powerful way to deliver your message. Look for creative ways to speak on your topic. It reduces the *homework* factor.

Summary

- **Last-minute tip:** Use the Quick Prep Method if you don't have much time to prepare a presentation. Write down the questions your audience would have, and prepare answers in bullet points.

■ **If you have more time:** Use the Audience Agenda System to write out what members of your audience want to know. Focus on their interests. Organize your presentation around what they want to know, not what you want to talk about.

■ **Plan for ongoing improvement:** Hire a graphic designer, and develop better slides, books, photos, and handouts for your presentations. Be creative. Use your imagination. It will pay off in the presentation.

11

Q&A Sessions: Thinking on Your Feet

"The important thing is not to stop questioning."

—ALBERT EINSTEIN, Nobel Prize Winner, Physics

IF YOU ARE THE leader of your organization, tough questions come your way. Employee meetings, board meetings, client meetings, media interviews, town meetings, legislative committees, panels, and public speeches all typically include Q&A sessions. Most of the Q&A is not that tough to handle. You know most of the answers. However, Q&A can be difficult because of controversy, privacy, litigation, sensitivity, pending decisions, mistakes, or misunderstandings.

Four Rules for Q&A Sessions

A leader's job is to answer the questions. In fact, a leader's job is to *invite* them. Questions give you a chance to manage the dialogue. Tough questions are better than no questions. If the room goes silent when you ask for questions, it is not a good sign. It may mean people are walking away with issues unresolved. Unresolved issues can undermine you later. You want to know what issues are lurking out there. Questions tell you what people are concerned about and give you a chance to respond.

So, as CEO, you learn to be glad when you get tough questions. That doesn't make every Q&A session pleasant. There are subjects you don't want to discuss. There are people who are difficult. That's why I have four rules for dealing with Q&A sessions:

1. Be calm.
2. Be honest.
3. Be available.
4. Be open-minded.

Be Calm

The cardinal rule—the number one concept to remember in any Q&A session, no matter the topic or the people—is to be calm. Keep your cool, no matter what. Control your emotion—manage the dialogue.

Paul Levy, CEO of Beth Israel Deaconess, was once the head of a state agency that was constantly under fire from the public and the press. The Massachusetts Water Resources Authority raised water rates to record levels and built water treatment facilities that people didn't want in their towns. Levy went into forum after forum to face tough questions. How did he survive?

"I just made it my rule to be polite and respectful. You have to understand that the reason you are there is to be yelled at," he said. "You address their concerns," he stressed. "You have to be professional, and you have to be empathetic."

Be Honest

"When in doubt, tell the truth."

—MARK TWAIN, American Writer

The second rule is to be honest. Honesty doesn't require work on your part. You say what you know within the bounds of what is legal, ethical, and appropriate. This way, you don't ever have to strive to *remember* what you said. In our survey, people said that the top qualities of communication they want from their bosses are honesty and integrity. People would rather hear the unvarnished truth than anything else.

Open the newspaper on any given day and you will find negative stories about companies that didn't tell the truth. Corporations and governments get into more hot water because of lies and cover-ups than because of mistakes. Mistakes people forgive. Lies they cannot tolerate. Leaders cannot afford to speak anything but the truth. There is too much at stake.

Telling the truth doesn't mean telling *all*. You must be judicious. In advance of any question-and-answer session, you should anticipate questions and prepare appropriate responses. If you cannot discuss something, it's perfectly acceptable to explain *why* you cannot. Privacy and litigation are common reasons. It's also acceptable to say you *do not know* something, *if* you don't. And, you are within your prerogative to explain that you cannot discuss something now, but to tell them *when you will* be able to discuss it. Handling tough questions with these methods is far better than misleading an audience. These methods will help you be judicious in Q&A sessions.

Be Available

The third principle for handling Q&A sessions is availability. As CEO, you can't answer the questions or manage the dialogue if you don't show up. One CEO makes it a point to hold town meetings at each of his company's four regional headquarters at least once a year. He speaks for about thirty minutes and then stays as long as several hours to answer employees' questions. There are a lot of benefits to this practice.

"I want to hear what's on their minds," the CEO said. "And just in case they aren't comfortable standing up to ask in front of a group, they can write their questions on a piece of paper before the meeting, and we make sure it is read."

If your company has more than one operating center, it can be challenging to make yourself available to everyone. The travel schedules of many CEOs are demanding. However, the effort is well worth it. Face-to-face forums with questions from employees, clients, or analysts can be one of the most valuable uses of your time.

Be Open-Minded

"The cure for boredom is curiosity. There is no cure for curiosity."

—Dorothy Parker, Author and Humorist

The fourth and final guideline for addressing audience questions is to be open-minded. Genuine curiosity will help you win over any audience. Curiosity gets you thinking about other people and allows you to really *hear* the question. You want to hear not just what they are saying but also what they are *feeling*. Listen for emotion. Pick up on the question behind the question. Get to the heart of the matter.

Open-mindedness can be challenging if *you* feel emotional about an issue. Once, I was coaching the top executive of a railroad company that was going through an investigation by the federal government. The executive believed the investigation was politically motivated, but to say so publicly would have made the situation worse. He wanted to get through it and put the whole thing behind them.

In answering questions during our practice session, he was defensive and closed. He crossed his arms and his voice got tight when we threw the predictable questions at him. It took two hours to get him to settle down and change his body language and tone of voice, but it was essential to diffuse the issue with the public and the press.

You will be more open to questions if you are well prepared for them. The next part of the chapter discusses how to prepare for any Q&A session. It offers a "patented" strategy to anticipate questions, as well as how to recognize types of difficult questions and how to trigger your brain to answer on the spot. Let's start with a method to anticipate questions: the 98 Percent Solution.

The 98 Percent Solution

You will be more confident and better prepared for Q&A sessions if you can anticipate the audience's questions. The 98 Percent Solution helps you prepare for *almost any question*. While it might be difficult to imagine everything an audience will want to know, most of the time the questions are obvious. It's your business—you live it and breathe it, and you should have a good idea what people are going to ask.

The 98 Percent Solution is really just learning to think like your toughest critics and most hard-nosed skeptics. Thinking the way they do allows you to move from a defensive posture to the offensive position. You come at it from their point of view, and you actually know what they're going to ask before they ask it. Knowing what they will ask allows you to effectively prepare.

To put the 98 Percent Solution into practice, write down the worst questions—the ones you don't want to answer. Don't bother to write down the questions you would like people to ask, because you already know the answers to those. Write down the questions you wish no one would ask, even the ones that make you cringe.

Once you have the tough questions on paper, start drafting your answers. I strongly believe in writing out your answers. This process tells you whether you need more information. Then, spend time phrasing the answer exactly as you would like to deliver it. By writing it out, you clarify and internalize the message.

Don't ever wing the answer to a question that involves litigation, privacy, sensitivity, a misunderstanding, or a mistake. Determine what you can say, as well as what you can't. If you cannot answer, explain why you can't. Explaining your reasons for not being able to speak is an extremely useful tool. Even a hostile audience has to respect a good reason why you cannot discuss something. You will find more advice on answering tough questions from the media in Chapter 12.

The Other 2 Percent

Even if you can anticipate 98 percent of the questions, 2 percent can surprise you. One way to deal with the unknown is to talk to members of the audience in advance. You can usually ferret out the surprises by calling the head of the organization in advance or by arriving early and talking face-to-face with people in the audience before the meeting starts.

"What works for me," said Paul Levy, "is to show up early and mingle with the crowd." Levy, who has turned around several bad situations in organizations he led, explained, "By arriving early, I get a sense of people and the current issues in their lives." If you want to know what people are thinking, ask. The best time to ask is *before* the meeting starts.

Types of Tough Questions

There are several distinct types of tough questions, and it's to your benefit to learn to recognize them. There is a strategy for handling each that you can use, once you've learn to spot them. The four primary types are the false alternative, the irrelevant, the hypothetical, and the anonymous question. Here is a brief look at each, with some advice on how to respond.

False Alternative

The false alternative presents two or more equally wrong or inaccurate answers from which you are asked to choose. Your course of action in fielding such a question is not to take the bait: refuse to accept either alternative, and set the record straight. Go to the root of the question. Be factual in your answer to refute what is implied in the false alternative. Here's an example:

> **Question:** *"Is your firm charging these rates because you just think you can get them, or because you are the only game in town?"*

> **Answer:** *"We have developed what we know is a fair, competitive fee structure based on the value of the service. Our costs have risen 5 percent, but our fees are going up only 3 percent."*

Irrelevant

This type of question is not closely connected to the topics of discussion. It takes you in a direction in which you do not want or need to go. You don't want to say, "No comment," or appear dismissive or defensive; you just want to move away from the issue because it is not relevant. The answer can be to suggest when, where, or who might be more appropriate for discussing the topic. You want to be helpful without getting trapped by an irrelevant question. For example:

> **Question:** *"Do you think men in our business should wear ties to work or not?"*

Your answer could acknowledge that the person feels the dress code is an issue but delegate the responsibility for answering. You are not the person making the rules on dress code, although you may direct that someone else handle it.

> **Answer:** *"It's an issue worth discussing in every organization. We want to project a professional image. I will ask the HR department to look into it, and we will let everyone know how we will proceed."*

Hypothetical

The hypothetical presents a situation that is unlikely to happen, too far in the future, or impossible to predict. However, this type of question is one you should welcome because it tells you what people are concerned about. For example:

> **Question:** *"If we lost these two big customers at the end of the year, would you lay off employees?"*

You must respect the person asking the question while pointing out the hypothetical situation: not likely, too far in the future, or impossible to predict.

> **Answer:** *"We have acknowledged the mistakes we've made with those customers and told them we are committed to excellence. If we commit to the plan, those customers will be with us next year."*

Anonymous Source

Sometimes people ask questions about rumors they have heard, and sometimes they use anonymous sources to pose questions they just want to ask. Anonymous source questions can be irritating, but you should welcome them, as well, for the light they shed on people's concerns. It is almost never a good idea to put the person asking the question on the spot and try to find out the source of the information. Doing that places the questioner in a defensive position and sets up the wrong dynamic. Example:

> **Question:** *"We are hearing rumors that we are going to merge with a bigger company—is our company in play?"*

Tell the truth, but deflect anything that is pure gossip.

> **Answer:** *"There is no truth to that statement; we are not in discussions about a merger."*

> **Or:** *"As I am sure each of you understands, we are not at liberty to discuss whether this company would consider such an offer, because of legal reasons, but if that does happen, you have my word that you will be fully informed. We are open and honest with employees about our business, and if there is such an opportunity, we will let you know at the appropriate time."*

What About Questions You Haven't Anticipated?

One of my clients was invited to interview for a prestigious White House fellowship: a one-year stint in Washington for accomplished professionals who could be policy advisers or political leaders someday. The interview process is rigorous: seven days of breakfasts, forums, panels, and receptions. Think of it as a weeklong, high-pressure job interview.

Since this woman had interviewed for a fellowship once before, she knew how tough it would be. In one particularly unnerving situation, former fellows have the opportunity to ask the candidates an absurd question. In the previous round of interviews, someone had asked her, "What is your opinion of Big Bird?" The point is to see how well these candidates think on their feet.

At first, answering such an absurd question may seem impossible. But there is a way to trigger your brain to do it. This Trigger Method, as I call it, will help you form a clear, succinct answer to any question on the spot. The Trigger Method works well because it signals your brain to go search for an answer. I have taught this method to dozens and dozens of clients, with excellent results.

The Trigger Method

You "trigger" your brain by beginning a sentence either with the end of the question or with a characterization. The first method, repeating the end of the question, triggers your brain to go hunting for information that's in there. The second method, beginning your sentence with a characterization, triggers your brain to form and deliver a reasonable opinion on a topic. Let's explore each of these methods and when you would use each.

Trigger 1: Repeat the End of the Question

Let's say someone in the audience asks you why you are raising the price of your product. You start your statement with the end of the question: "We are raising the price of the product because . . ."; your brain then goes searching for the answer. What pops up is, " . . . our costs have risen." By repeating the question as a statement at the beginning of your answer, you trigger your brain to search—and in a split second, you have an answer. You are also speaking in a complete sentence, which makes you sound clear and confident. So, start with the key phrase in your answer, and fill in the blank. You will never look lost, stammer through an answer, or appear unsure if you use this method.

To try this out, write down a few of the tough questions you typically get, and then use the method. Speaking out loud, take the key phrase of the question and put it at the beginning of the sentence. You should find that your brain kicks right into gear, which allows you to deliver a clear, thoughtful answer.

Trigger 2: Make a Qualifying or Opinion Statement

Let's say someone in the audience asks your opinion about an issue. Here you can employ a different kind of trigger. What you are really being ask to do is to characterize an issue. So, you start with a characterization. You trigger you brain to come up with an answer by beginning your sentence with a characterizing phrase. For example, if someone is asking your opinion about a movie, you could start by saying, "The best thing about the movie . . . ," or, "The worst thing about the movie . . . "; either way, you trigger your brain to go searching for what you thought was the best, or the worst, aspect.

Starting the sentence tells your brain to search. You can usually fill in the blank immediately. You will be amazed at how quickly you can retrieve a reasonable opinion. "The best thing about the movie was Dustin Hoffman's performance." "The worst thing about the movie was the lack of character development." Start the sentence with the qualifying statement and you will trigger your brain to instantly supply the appropriate words.

Here are a few examples of triggers that will help you deliver opinion effectively. Start with one of these statements, and fill in the blank. It works like magic.

- The best thing about _____ is _____.
- The most critical thing to remember about _____ is
  _____.
- The most important aspect of _____ is _____.
- What excites me about _____ is _____.
- The worst thing about _____ is _____.
- The most disturbing aspect of _____ is _____.
- The most distressing _____.
- What troubles me about _____ is _____.
- The one thing you must do/know/believe is _____.
- The most unique thing about _____ is _____.

- The most provocative, or thought-provoking, aspect of _____ is _____.
- What is interesting about _____ is _____.
- Contrary to what _____ believe(s), _____.

You can try this right now. Pick an object in the room where you are sitting. It can be anything: a chair, a picture, a pen—anything you can see. What do you think of that chair? Pause, and use a "trigger" statement to start your answer. This is an oral exercise. Do it out loud. Don't write it out. We're training your brain to quickly respond to a question.

Triggers work. If you start well, you end well. You speak in complete sentences. This is especially effective in media interviews. Triggers keep you from making a false start or stammering through an answer. Practice these and they will become second nature.

More Tips for Answering Tough Questions

- **Be gracious.** Tough questions are meant to test how you manage pressure. A leader must always be calm, cool, and gracious under pressure.

- **Be positive.** No one wants to be around a negative person. The job of a leader is to be honest, but do look at the bright side whenever possible.

- **Be brief.** Too many details can be dull. It's better to give a short answer—and read the audience to see if they want more—than to talk too long and lose them.

- **Be complete.** Don't commit the sin of omission. Omitting facts or important elements of the answer is just as bad as not telling the truth.

- **Be specific.** Give examples if necessary. If you're too vague, you sound evasive. You can be specific without giving too much detail—the detail should be relevant.

■ **Be strategic.** Think about how you can turn a negative into a positive, or how you can use a question to promote a value that is important.

Summary

■ **Last-minute tip:** Use the Trigger Method to answer a tough question on the fly. When asked your opinion about something, start by saying, "The best thing about X is Y."

■ **If you have more time:** Use the 98 Percent Solution to prepare for your next meeting. Write down the toughest questions you'll get from your skeptics and critics.

■ **Plan for ongoing improvement:** Identify areas in which you could improve when answering questions. Incorporate those in your coaching plan. For example, if you need to give shorter answers, turn on your internal editor; pay attention to your intuition. If you are asking yourself whether an answer was too long, it probably was.

12

Media Interviews

"Authenticity in the age of media isn't just half the battle;
it's a real achievement, a triumph almost."

—PEGGY NOONAN, Speechwriter

MEDIA INTERVIEWS ARE INTIMIDATING for most people, including CEOs. Facing the unknown is disquieting. If we are unprepared, even the friendliest reporters can ruffle us with unexpected questions. And the tougher reporters who try to coax, wheedle, browbeat, bully, or coerce can make anyone regret having come to work today. You can't be a leader in any organization without developing some media savvy.

Media savvy is a requirement whether you are talking to members of the mainstream, business, or trade press. You are the voice and face of the company. Your words ripple out like a wave, often creating a seismic force, whether the news is good or bad. Your employees, customers, competitors, directors, analysts, and public are listening. If your company is public, you also have the ears of the business press, the stock exchanges, and government regulators. So, you must know what you're doing.

With so many media outlets, you can't fly under the radar even if you want to. In recent years, we've all seen the proliferation of twenty-four-hour news programs, radio talk shows, and news websites, as well as business and trade publications. This means there are inevitably more reporters out looking for stories and interviews. As CEO, you will be on their radar screens whether you like it or not. While many companies have a policy not to speak to the press, a policy like that can create suspicion and backfire.

There are legitimate reasons not only to be responsive but also to actively seek out the media. Positive press is powerful. You can generate goodwill with your key audiences. People believe a large percentage of what they see and hear in the press. Unlike advertising, it isn't bought and paid for. So, seeking out press is good business. You want to learn more than how to handle press inquiries. You need a strategy to send out a positive message.

Creating a strategy includes training all the key people in your organization to talk to the press. There are only two ways to learn: media training and real-life experience. Charlie Baker, CEO of Harvard Pilgrim Health Care, faced the press for eight years in government before he became CEO. "You get a lot of practice, opportunities to learn from mistakes—and that was good for me," he says. Spending time in the public eye also helped Baker learn how to avoid generating negative press. According to Baker, "You screw up in that environment and you're on the evening news."

I've been on both sides of the microphone—as a reporter and as an expert being interviewed by reporters. I can tell you I prefer doing the asking. But the answering side can be tolerable, even enjoyable, if you develop media skills. Media training will teach you more than how *not* to answer questions. You will learn to anticipate questions, prepare properly, and convey your message in a clear, confident way. If you can do this, you can handle any media interview.

Larry Lucchino, who has been CEO of three major-league baseball teams, acquired the Boston Red Sox with two partners in 2002. Lucchino, TV magnate Tom Werner, and Wall Street financier John Henry went to work immediately to court the press. Although this storied franchise had some of the most devoted fans in baseball, that devotion had not always translated into TV ratings. But through their press efforts, two years before winning the World Series in 2004, these new owners successfully boosted the team's local TV audience. They had the highest local TV ratings in the country, due to their combined media savvy.

Lucchino enjoys repartee with sports reporters on TV and radio and in print. He's funny and direct. He says that the best advice he's received about media relations came from former Red Sox owner Hayward Sullivan: "When Hayward was walking to the first press conference with us, he told me, 'Be honest. There are so many (reporters), they'll find out if you're not.'" Lucchino knows what it takes to make a good interview. "It's a lot like sex or dancing," he said. "It takes two to do it well."

On-Camera Presence

More and more, you will be *seen*, as well as heard. In addition to television, there are many other high-visibility venues where you must project an image of leadership. You may deliver a speech from a podium shown on a big screen in a ballroom. Perhaps you'll record a streaming-video message to employees. Maybe you'll attend meetings via videoconference across time zones and continents. Being on camera is not just about being on CNBC. Cameras are everywhere.

Whether you are talking to television, radio, newspaper, or magazine reporters, you will be more successful if you understand what they want. What are they looking for when they call for an interview? All reporters are looking for news; they want to know what's new. If you understand how they determine what is newsworthy, you will be more prepared to give a better interview.

What's News?

Here are a few attributes reporters have in mind when seeking out a story:

- **Timeliness**—if it's happening now, it's news
- **Trends**—a lot of people are doing it, seeing it, or experiencing it
- **Controversy**—debate sells newspapers and gets people to listen and watch
- **Expertise**—special knowledge of the topic, succinct and interesting

- **Strong opinions**—clear statements about a position or situation
- **Fresh angles**—a new twist on an ongoing issue or problem
- **Broad appeal**—especially to their target viewers, listeners, or readers

Interview Strategies

One of the core strategies for managing an interview is anticipating the questions. It isn't as difficult as you may imagine to know what reporters will ask. The strategy to use is the 98 Percent Solution, explained in Chapter 11. With this strategy, you write down the worst questions you expect from your toughest critics. Put yourself in the skeptics' shoes—imagine what they would ask. For the average interview, you should be writing down at least ten to twenty questions that you may be asked.

Have you noticed that some of the most well-known, experienced experts and commentators sound as if they always know what the hosts are going to ask? They seem to have an answer ready, no matter what the question, and they respond with insight and wit. Most of those analysts are intuitively using the 98 Percent Solution. Many spend hours preparing so that they sound brilliant "off-the-cuff." It's true that in some cases they have been "prepped" by producers. But through experience they can pretty much figure out what the host will ask. They do their research and even write out witty lines or try them on colleagues before the program. Of course, there are plenty of analysts and commentators who are downright brilliant on the fly. But most of the time, they have anticipated most of the questions. And you can take a page out of their book.

It's imperative to write down the questions you expect. Doing so kicks your brain into gear and helps you formulate a strong, clear answer to the question. You or someone on your staff should think like a reporter and start jotting down the probing questions that get to the heart of the issue. You can never, ever be too prepared for an interview. If they don't ask some of those questions, at least you were ready. I believe that writing down the questions is even more valuable than preparing talking points for an interview.

The other strategy you can use to give better interviews is also covered in Chapter 11: the Trigger Method. This technique allows you to "trigger" your brain to fire out an answer to a question by starting with an element of the question. You can also trigger the brain to deliver opinion by beginning with a characterization, such as "the best thing" or "the worst thing." The triggers tell your brain to hunt for information that is stored there. Triggers enable you to speak in complete sentences and keep your answer focused. You can practice again by reviewing the previous chapter.

Be Responsive

From the moment a call comes from a reporter, a producer, or an editor, you should respond in some way. Reporters appreciate and remember when you pick up the phone and appear open. Even if you do not want to comment on an issue, it is a good idea for one of your media-savvy colleagues to respond and be as helpful as possible. You can suggest another source for a story or provide a statement, policy papers, or articles on the issue. You can refer the reporter to other experts who can speak in general terms on a topic. You may simply tell the reporter why you can't talk to the media about an issue, for any legitimate reason: a pending decision, litigation, privacy, or other restraints.

You do not have to respond, but someone from your organization should. Have the designee politely return the call within a reasonable time, and decline in a friendly way, *always*. The reason for adopting this approach is that your company's public attitude with the reporter will be noted. You don't want to convey the impression that you have something to hide. You can wrongly leave that impression by not being responsive. You want to maintain good relations with as many reporters as possible. The next time, you may *want* to do the interview.

Sometimes you get calls for interviews that will be beneficial to you and your organization. Advise the person who is taking press calls to ask about the deadline. Even if the deadline is coming up right away, always put off the interview, if just briefly. That will give you a chance to prepare to give an outstanding interview. Anticipate questions and jot down talking points. Give yourself at least fifteen minutes—an hour or two, if possible. Use that time well. *Even if you think you are ready*, it never hurts to craft a good quote or two. A pithy, interesting observation will help you get quoted and maximize the value of the interview.

You can ask reporters to give you a general idea of the questions they will ask. Most will comply. They won't give you *all* the questions, because one topic or question leads to new questions. If they're doing their jobs well, they will follow the thread of the conversation. You would expect any competent reporter to do that.

Once you've set up the time for the interview, write down all the questions you think you might get—even the ones you don't want to be asked. Then, you and/or your communications person can list some talking points: three ideas, concepts, or facts that you want to share in this interview.

Prepare Talking Points

Talking points are a shorthand script from which to work during an interview. Typically, you want to try to convey two or three primary messages. Those messages should be clear, concise, and *interesting*—something people don't know or may not have considered. Reporters are looking for what's new or trendy, and you can be quoted if you can give it to them.

One way to come up with interesting talking points is to analyze an issue from different angles. Consider how some people view it versus others. Another point of interest can be a startling fact: something most people don't know. This is stuff you probably run across every day in your reading and conversations in your industry.

The media also like to hear opinions. When you have an opinion, share it. This helps establish you as a thought leader in your industry. Be sure your opinion positions you and your organization in a positive way. Don't give an opinion that jeopardizes your business or reputation.

When explaining difficult concepts, make them clear. Use analogies and descriptive language. Provide examples. Do your best to help the interviewer fully understand. Your task is to be sure the reporter understands well enough to write the story for the average reader or viewer.

If someone else has prepared the talking points, be sure to review them before your interview. Edit the remarks if necessary so that you're speaking in your own voice. You want to sound conversational, and the best way to do that is to edit and become familiar with the talking points.

Practice Out Loud

You should practice your delivery. You will do a better job if you are primed. It can be difficult to address the questions and incorporate your talking points unless you practice. One of the biggest frustrations for PR firms and VPs of communications, whether inside or outside the company, is handing over talking points to a CEO who never really looks at them before dialing the reporter's number.

The consequence of not reviewing the talking points and practicing out loud is that the interview rarely goes as hoped. You can be misquoted, or just missing from the story, if you don't work in your talking points smoothly and make the interview lively and interesting. Can you always avoid being misquoted? I'll tell you, it's almost impossible. Reporters are human beings, and they make mistakes. However, you will have a better shot at conveying your points if you practice out loud. If you are misquoted, you can ask for a correction, but few readers notice them.

"Flag" Messages

A flag is a verbal cue that you are about to say something significant. "The most important thing to remember is . . . " and "The most valuable lesson here is . . . " are examples of flags. Reporters listen for these verbal cues and edit accordingly. If you want reporters to notice an idea, start the sentence with a flag. Reporters on deadline will listen for those cues and drop in the quotes or sound bites.

You can also use flags to correct any misperception or factual error in a reporter's question or comment. For example, if you are asked a question that contains erroneous information, you can say, "It's interesting that such a perception developed, but let me clear something up. It's important to know that . . . ," or, "What actually happened is . . . ." By flagging the idea, you will call attention to it and enable the reporter to follow your thoughts more easily.

Build "Bridges"

A conversation bridge takes you from the first part of an answer to a key point. Bridges are similar to flags, but you use them in the middle of an answer to move from a topic the interviewer has raised to one that you want to emphasize. I want to stress that bridges are not supposed to be used to avoid answering a question. They are only a strategy for managing the interview and making sure you get to make your points, too.

After you respond to the question, you use some connecting language to bridge to your key points. For example, you can use phrases such as "What's important to remember" or "The critical decision" or "What we're happy to report" and follow with your talking points. Remember, *don't ignore the question*; use the bridge to move the conversation forward. Reporters actually appreciate it when you answer the question and then take the conversation a step further. That adds value and reduces some of the work of interviewing. In a live interview, a bridge is an effective way to make sure you say what you came to say.

Use Your Voice

Your voice is a powerful tool in media interviews. By using your voice effectively, you guide reporters to the important stuff. Your tone, inflection, emphasis, pace, and timing will help them pick up on what is important. If you're not sure how your voice sounds, record it while you are practicing for an interview. Reporters replaying the tape of your actual interview later will be listening for *vocal* cues as well as *verbal* ones.

Be Brief

"The trouble with me is that I like to talk too much."
—WILLIAM HOWARD TAFT, 27th U.S. President

It's a good thing that President Taft didn't live in the age of television — he might never have been elected. These days, leaders have to speak with the eloquence of a statesman, in a nanosecond.

I recently timed a thirty-minute national newscast on NBC to see whether the familiar term "fifteen-second sound bite" was accurate. Over my years in journalism, it seemed that interviews were getting shorter. Even I was shocked when I calculated the average and found that it was only *seven seconds*, and many "sound bites" were only two or three seconds long.

Brevity is important not only on television but also on radio and even in print. Count the number of words in a quote on the front page of your newspaper or in a weekly or monthly magazine. Five to twelve words is pretty common.

Never Say, "No Comment"

The worst thing you can ever say to a reporter is, "No comment." You come across as defensive and guilty. If you are asked a question that you don't want to answer, explain why you can't. Whether it's privacy, a legal matter, or any other legitimate reason, reporters will be satisfied with an *acceptable* explanation.

Ari Fleischer, press secretary for George Bush, gave three hundred White House press briefings during two and a half years that included the September 11 terrorist attacks and the wars in Afghanistan and Iraq. In a good-bye interview with Juan Williams, of NPR, Fleischer shared revealing insights about how to say enough, and not too much, without using "No comment." Here's an excerpt from that interview:

Williams: So, I heard you describe (a White House press) briefing as "intellectual chess."

Fleischer: Yes.

Williams: The president, in an interview, when I asked about you, once said, "Ari Fleischer knows the difference between knowing and saying."

Fleischer: I mean, things move so fast that I'm in the room for much of what he does, and that includes many of his summits, or

> most of his summit meetings—all his domestic and economic policy briefings. And so I get to hear a lot of what the president thinks and why he thinks it.
>
> **Williams:** He even said that you were on the phone when he's talking to some foreign leaders. I was surprised to hear that.
>
> **Fleischer:** That's correct. That'll happen from time to time, particularly on the most newsworthy calls, because I know the press is going to want to know what he talked about. Doing that, everything I say must—must—be truthful, and it always has been. But everything that's truthful does not need to be said.

It's just as important for you, as a CEO, to learn to be skillful in answering, without saying, "No comment." Don't say anything you don't want to see in print, but don't fall back on "No comment"—it will just make matters worse.

You're *Always* on the Record

Ann Murphy, a veteran news journalist who now helps CEOs with public relations, says that one of the biggest mistakes CEOs make is saying things to reporters that they can't take back. "They have to understand that what you say is on the record," says Ann. "You can be led in a different direction and end up talking about things you don't want to talk about."

Ann has observed that some CEOs think they know how to talk to the media, but when they wake up the next morning and read their quotes in the paper, they are shocked. She points out, "If you choose to say something, and they quote it, your PR person can't go take it back. The only things a PR person can correct are factual errors."

Assume the Microphone Is On

In March 2004, Senator John Kerry was talking off-the-cuff with supporters at the conclusion of a speech on tax cuts in Chicago. He didn't realize that his "off-camera" remarks were being recorded as the cameras

shot video of him shaking hands. "These guys (the Republican administration) are the most crooked, you know, lying group I've ever seen," said
Kerry, and it made all the nightly newscasts. George Bush was also caught
with a hot microphone in September 2000 before a campaign speech in
Illinois when he made what he thought was a private comment to Dick
Cheney about a certain reporter in the crowd. "There's Adam Clymer,
major league asshole from the *New York Times*," Bush said. His comment
was recorded and later hit the newscasts.

Anything you don't want to appear in print or on TV, don't say
within a mile of a microphone, even if someone has assured you that the
microphone is turned off. Rookie mistakes with microphones have gotten the best of many savvy media people who should know better.

Be Patient

Reporters are not experts in your field. They are generalists by design.
Their editors don't want them to be experts on what you do. Reporters
are moved from beat to beat to keep them fresh. If they understand too
much, they will not explain things well to their readers, viewers, and listeners. Familiarity can be deadly for reporters. So, don't be impatient
when you have to explain. Give them the background they need to write
a good story, and be sure they leave with all of their questions answered.
You may also want to invite reporters who are new to your industry for a
background briefing and help them get up to speed on the issues. I know
several CEOs who have done this and found it helps them to help the
reporters.

Don't Overreact

You may feel angry, frustrated, impatient, or defensive during an interview. Keep it in check. Above all, avoid engaging in hostility. For a leader,
there is no upside to taking the bait.

Rehearse the answers to difficult questions with a media expert or
PR person. Use videotape, or get expert feedback on your choice of words
and tone of voice; everything from voice to facial expression and body
language can give away how you are feeling.

Handling a Media Crisis

A crisis is an event, revelation, allegation, or set of circumstances that threatens the integrity, reputation, or survival of an individual or institution. FYI: It doesn't have to be true—it simply has to be public, or have the potential to be public, and cause harm.

The rules of crisis communication are to be responsive, honest, and concerned. You must respond even if the facts are not all in, because they never really are. Honesty is imperative, because you can create a secondary crisis if you fib. You have to show concern, because people will forgive and forget if they know you care.

Generally, you should give an interview in a crisis as soon as possible, so you can control the message. If you don't, you leave a vacuum that the media can fill with imaginings. "I learned early on that even if this news isn't great, you have to be the first to tell the story," says Sovereign Bank of New England chairman John Hamill. "If you are acting, rather than reacting, it's better; at least then you won't be the subject of an ongoing investigation of what happened," he observed. "You only get one shot, and once the TV or radio goes on, or the reporter leaves, that's it. So, you get your story in there as best and as quickly as you can, or you suffer the consequences."

Rules of Crisis Communication

- **Anticipate issues.** Stay ahead of the curve so you can be prepared with answers to reporters' questions.

- **Get out front.** When you have something to say, say it before the media find someone who will discuss the issue or its repercussions.

- **Act; don't react.** Once you react, you are in a defensive posture. Tell people ahead of time what you are doing, what will happen, or what they can expect.

- **Be visible.** Don't hide. Even if you have nothing to say, be available; when you are invisible, the media assume there is a reason.

- **Tell the truth.** This is the cardinal rule of rules. Always tell the truth. The truth is easy. Lies you have to remember, and the truth always comes out anyway.

- **Fully inform spokespersons.** Don't keep the people who need to talk to the media in the dark. Have people you trust and who know "the difference between knowing and saying."

- **Talk directly with stakeholders.** Make sure everyone who is integral to your business is fully informed by you or your organization and doesn't get the news about your company indirectly from the media.

- **Express empathy and concern.** This is the second most important rule, next to honesty. If you express genuine concern for others—even if you are in a dispute—you will probably be forgiven.

- **Take responsibility.** Owning a problem, especially as the leader, is one of the secrets to defusing a crisis. You are more likely to be forgiven for making a mistake if you apologize and make amends.

- **Don't delay.** You can shape the discussion and use the media to transmit your message. Delays can create a secondary crisis.

Summary

- **Last-minute tip:** Wait fifteen minutes to call a reporter back so that you have time to draft your talking points. This will help you manage the interview and ensure that you say the things you want to say.

- **If you have more time:** Work on your on-camera presence by practicing interviews on videotape. You need to develop this presence not only for television but also for streaming videos, speeches with cameras, and videoconferencing.

- **Plan for ongoing improvement:** Develop a crisis plan for your organization that includes media training for you and the key spokespersons of your organization. Everyone should know the principles of crisis communication and be ready to give interviews. I hope you never have a crisis, but if you do, you will be prepared.

13

Leading Meetings

*"Leadership is the art of getting someone else to do
something you want done because he wants to do it."*
—DWIGHT D. EISENHOWER, 34th U.S. President

BY THE TIME YOU become CEO, you will have led a lot of meetings. But
as CEO, you set the meeting standard. Your meeting leadership style
establishes the tone and influences the meeting culture. People take their
cues from you, adopting your practices—good and bad.

Even when you are not leading the meeting, you influence it. Your
presence changes the dynamic of the meeting simply because you are
there. As one CEO told me, "The one individual who participates in
every single meeting, and leads most of them, is the CEO."

Businesses have to run meetings, but often, meetings run businesses. In many organizations, meeting management has run amuck.
Meetings are called back-to-back; they start late, lose focus, erupt in personal conflict, accomplish little, and leave no one accountable. It is up to
the CEO to exert influence to make meetings productive. Your meeting
habits, policies, and management training determine the effectiveness of
meetings in the organization.

It's remarkable how many meetings some people attend. Some say
there are so many meetings that they have no time to do their work. It

should come as no surprise that surveys show that people hate meetings. One client tells me people in her office "do leg lifts and dig their nails into the palms of their hands just to stay awake."

"I have strong feelings about how meetings should be run," said Talbots CEO Arnold Zetcher. "You have to keep everyone on topic and keep it moving. It's easy to get sidetracked." However, if your meetings are all business, that too can backfire. It's about balance. "People need to enjoy the time they are there. I try to inject a little humor to help people have fun," said Arnold.

As a result of interviews with CEOs, my company drew up a list of best meeting practices—what the leaders say works. While there are different meeting styles, certain practices and policies make meetings better.

Different types of meetings require different approaches. You may not run meetings of your senior team the way you run meetings of fifty or more employees in the cafeteria. Be flexible and adapt to the purpose of the meeting and the participants and follow these practices:

Meeting Leader Competencies
- Writing a good, working agenda
- Identifying issues before the meeting
- Getting buy-in from stakeholders in advance
- Encouraging discussion and participation
- Starting, staying, and ending on time
- Managing conflict
- Actively listening
- Summarizing points
- Building consensus
- Motivating others
- Creating accountability

Premeeting Decisions

Successful meetings start *before* the meeting. You have to decide whether to have a meeting, who should be invited, what to put on the agenda, and how to win support or uncover objections in advance.

The first decision is always whether to have a meeting. Some meetings are unnecessary. Answering the following questions can help you decide whether to have a meeting:

- What issues could be handled without a meeting?
- What would happen if we did not have the meeting at all?
- What would happen if we postponed the meeting?

The next decision is who should be at the meeting. One CEO is a real stickler about this. Only those who actually will make contributions to the discussion are invited to his meetings. No one is there to observe, learn, or be kept in the loop. The CEO believes the only way to streamline the meeting culture is to make sure that when people attend meetings, they are there for a reason. People in the organization appreciate that respect for their time.

Here are some questions you can ask to decide on participation:

- Who has the information we need to discuss?
- Who needs to make the decisions?
- Who needs to execute the plan?
- Who else is absolutely essential to the success of this project or meeting?

Creating an Agenda

An agenda is a primary meeting tool. It sets expectations, keeps meetings on track, and creates accountability. In an ideal world, every meeting should have an agenda, even if it is a simple one. I hear time and time again from people who attend meetings without agendas that meeting missions fall by the wayside—participants talk about whatever is on their minds instead.

Once people endure a few of these meetings, they get discouraged. If they can get away with it, they won't show up for the next one—or worse, they will find out later that they should have attended a meeting because of the topic. Without an agenda, participants cannot prepare properly, so time is lost while people read or catch up. Without an agenda, it is easy for one or two people to hijack the meeting. As the meeting wanders, people start to whisper in side conversations. The meetings end before decisions are made, or decisions are made after people have left. It all adds up to low morale and high frustration.

Paul Levy, CEO of Beth Israel Deaconess Medical Center, a Harvard teaching hospital, says, "You have to have an agenda. You have to clearly state whether it's information or a decision you want."

To make your agenda effective and to avoid the problems previously discussed, here's a smart way to proceed:

- Give the meeting a title.
- Briefly describe the purpose.
- Name the participants.
- State briefly but precisely the aspects of each pertinent issue.
- Delineate impending decisions.
- Write in the time limit for each item (and stick to it).
- Include hidden agenda items that could derail the meeting if they need discussion.
- Distribute reading materials in advance with the agenda.
- Confirm that participants received the agenda at least twenty-four hours in advance.
- Allow time for participation and discussion.

Premeeting Communication

Productive meetings start with premeeting communication. You may need to ask questions of participants, discuss an issue, and get feedback or even buy-in in advance. Having discussions with influential people who will attend enables you to identify issues and take the temperature of the group. You find out where there is consensus and where you need to spend time, even before the meeting starts.

Several days or even weeks before a meeting, you may want to check in with stakeholders and others who can influence outcomes by walking down the hall for a visit, calling them, or sending e-mails. Your objectives include the following:

- Let them know what's happening.
- Get their feedback on issues of concern.
- Pose questions.
- Gather information.
- Uncover new issues.
- Discuss options.
- Reach agreement about an approach or action.

Try this exercise. Ask yourself these questions prior to the meeting:

- Who can help you and why?
- Who can undermine the meeting's mission and why?
- What questions do you need to ask each attendee?
- What will you do with the information you obtain?

Encourage Participation

Discussion is highly regarded by top CEOs. Your most valuable resource is the collective knowledge and intellect of your employees. One CEO told me he encourages people to raise objections by taking note of who is quiet and making it a point to ask them what they think. "Sometimes I take a vote and tell them they cannot abstain. I think you have to confront the silence. You don't want those who disagree to walk out and undermine you later," he said.

A good leader encourages participation. Participation is essential to harnessing the creative power of your organization. When you encourage participation, everyone benefits. You cannot afford to let a few individuals dominate the conversation. You must make it safe and easy for everyone—even the quiet ones—to get involved.

Here are some examples of constructions a CEO can use to promote participation:

- "Maureen, you shook your head. What else do we need to consider?"
- "I would like to hear from Bill on this."
- "Jack, you and I talked about something before the meeting. Would you share it?"
- "Do we have all the issues on the table?"
- "Is there anything else we need to consider?"
- "What don't we know that we need to know?"
- "Is there anyone who hasn't weighed in on this issue?"

Stimulate Discussion

Your language and tone of voice are tools you can use to stimulate discussion. Don't give your opinion first; let others speak. Tell them you want to hear from them. Make eye contact, and ask people questions. For example:

- "What's your reaction . . . ?"
- "What's your view of . . . ?"
- "How do you see . . . ?"
- "What led you to . . . ?"
- "What are some other ideas . . . ?"
- "How could we . . . ?"

One CEO says he always asks the group this question: "What do I need to know that I do not know?" That one question has made a big impact on the organization. Not only does he hear what he might not otherwise hear, but also people know that they can say what needs to be said, without retribution.

Manage Time

A chief complaint about meetings is that they start late, end late, and waste time in between. You can radically change the meeting culture of an organization simply by starting and ending on time. People will be much happier going to a meeting and will participate more fully if they know their time will be respected and they will accomplish what they came to do.

Often when new employees join an organization, they are dismayed by meeting practices. Those accustomed to punctual, efficient meetings quickly learn there's no point in being on time in the new company. They will be rewarded by sitting alone in a room, waiting for the rest of the crowd to roll in. Good employees become less effective because the culture works against them. The only way to make it work for everyone is to insist on good practices across the board, and good practices begin with starting on time.

Manage Conflict

Every leader knows that positive, healthy conflict is beneficial to an organization. You want to promote discussion, bring out issues, and hear viewpoints before making decisions. A meeting leader has to promote positive conflict while avoiding negative, personal attacks or vitriol that poison the work atmosphere and impede progress.

When a meeting leader asks insightful questions and makes it safe to disagree, participants will debate issues on the merits. If a meeting leader allows the discussion to get personal or lets issues go unresolved, conflict becomes personal. This damages the whole organization, not just the individuals involved. Meeting leaders must promote positive conflict while avoiding personal attacks.

Tips for Promoting Positive Conflict
- Create a safe, open environment.
- Encourage all participants to speak up.
- Use decision devices such as pros and cons, evaluation sheets, and grids.
- Set the ground rules and enforce them.

Tips for Managing Negative Conflict
- Listen to views.
- Identify common goals.

- Build on agreements.
- Avoid placing blame.
- Depersonalize through your own words.
- Look for a win-win outcome.
- Communicate respect.
- Use a positive tone.
- If conflict persists, take the issue off-line.
- Maintain zero tolerance for personal attacks.

Summarize Effectively

The ability to summarize points sets great leaders apart from the rest. The ability to summarize is, in essence, the ability to listen well and provide a brief but accurate review of what has been said. To summarize effectively, you must make it a habit to listen to everything, including what is said between the lines. You must also have a command of language and the ability to clarify concepts in order to sum up the main points of a discussion.

Following are some excellent ways to enhance your summarizing ability:

- Take notes or listen with a "note-taking" mind-set.
- Mentally capture key words and phrases.
- Repeat key words and phrases.
- Put individual ideas into the context of the whole discussion.
- Create analogies or "names" for central ideas.

Get to Consensus

Your goal in most meetings is to gather enough information to make a decision on your own, to get a consensus on a course of action, or to take a vote. Consensus builds in accountability and helps ensure that people act on decisions. Consensus does not imply an absence of conflict; it is the *resolution* of conflict in a way that is acceptable to a majority of participants.

To get to a consensus, you must take the following actions:

- Define the issue.
- Wait until others have spoken before offering your opinion.
- Encourage creative brainstorming.
- Assume responsibility for narrowing the options.
- Refrain from dominating discussion.
- Ask probing questions.
- Discuss the conflicts until issues are completely understood by everyone.
- Analyze and evaluate what you have learned.
- Summarize what has been said.
- Call for a decision, or make one.

Dealing with Difficult People

People who argue with you or talk among themselves can take a meeting off track in a hurry. While debate is usually healthy for organizations, some people in the group will test the limits. They will argue minuscule points, overlook others' views, or fail to recognize the value of compromise. They may be angry about something else or may feel ignored by the boss. They may be poor listeners. They may have hidden agendas. Most of the time, difficult people are not aware of how much they are irritating others, or what a serious impact they are having on their own careers as well as on the effectiveness of their teams.

You can avoid many of the problems that difficult people bring to the meeting by intervening in advance. Initiate a one-on-one conversation, acknowledging a known issue and allowing them to vent or discuss. Point out both the behavior you appreciate and the behavior that does not work. During the meeting itself, allow them to have their say, and even ask a few questions, and then move on. Enforce time limits. Tell the leaders of your organization to do the same.

Controlling Side Meetings

Side meetings are another problem in many meeting cultures. Sometimes side meetings happen simply because they are tolerated. Sometimes it's because the scheduled meetings get sidetracked or go too long. If people are bored or restless, they will have side meetings, unaware of how rude they are or how their behavior affects others.

You can't have a productive meeting when there are other meetings going on. The best way to handle this situation is by gradually escalating your intervention. First, look at the people talking until you catch their eyes. If they don't get the message, get up and walk over to them, or call on them. You may also want to remind the group of the meeting rules if you have a prohibition against side talking. By the time you reach this stage of intervention, everyone should have gotten the message. If some people haven't, pull them aside after the meeting. Make it clear that this kind of behavior cannot help them or the team.

The remainder of the chapter features more guidance from CEOs on how to make meetings work.

Be Open to Bad News

Some leaders *say* they want to hear bad news, but some really *mean* it. Phil Lussier is president of a division of Institutional Division, Citistreet, a large retirement plan management company. Phil is known as a good listener who's able to handle any news, favorable or unfavorable. One VP of the company told me, "Phil never gets upset or angry; he's always calm. He can hear twelve bad things in a row and will still have the same, calm manner."

As CEO, you too should create this kind of open atmosphere in meetings, especially if you think the news is bad. Lussier said, "It's important not to fall in love with your own ideas. And people should know they can say *anything*. That's very important."

Once people see others speaking up and delivering bad news without fear of consequences, they will feel OK about doing it, too. You may want to state that policy regularly to make sure people get the message.

Shake Things Up

Dan Wolf, CEO and founder of Cape Air, has an approach to shaking things up so meetings don't get stale. With his senior staff, he invites a different leader to facilitate each meeting. This helps them learn how to run meetings and keeps people on their toes.

"I believe process defines outcomes. If your process is stale, your outcomes will be stale," Dan says. Each team member has a different style, which prevents the group from falling into a rut. "Changing the dynamic doesn't make people *comfortable* all the time, but we're not striving for comfortable: we are striving for people to maximize their potential," he stresses.

There are many ways to shake things up. One of the most powerful ways is to change where you meet. A new venue can be like a breath of fresh air. You can also change the time that you meet. Another option is bring in outside facilitators. You may want to solicit suggestions for change from the group, especially if you see that your meetings are going stale.

Adopt the One-Page Memo

The amount of reading that people have to do to prepare for meetings can be staggering. Roger Marino, of EMC, says, "I had a rule at EMC. I worked for a couple of Harvard graduates, so I had to convince them not to use these twelve-, thirteen-, and fourteen-page reports on topics that didn't deserve it. I mean, who wants to read it? The person who does read it loses the *idea*, because it takes so long to read."

If you write a memo (and you should be judicious about writing them), it should be *one page*. And anyone preparing written material for meetings should know how to write. If you have staff members who don't know how to write, send them to a course, or provide a writing workshop. Executive coaches can also help with writing skills. Let people know that you value brevity. Insist on executive summaries of reports. Insist on good writing in e-mails, too. Your organization will run a lot more efficiently if people learn to write well. Imagine the time that you could save if memos were cut in half.

Give Nagging Rights

Tom Goemaat is president and CEO of Shawmut Design and Construction, whose clients include Harvard, MIT, Cheesecake Factory, Hermes, and Chanel. Tom believes in open meetings with employees, sharing as much about the company's financials and business status as he can. Before, during, or after a meeting, employees have "nagging rights," which means they can raise an issue with anyone—even the CEO—on any action that is not in concert with the company's core values.

"Some project managers came to us and said that we weren't treating our subcontractors fairly," said Tom. "Our core value was to treat subcontractors the same as employees. Nagging rights raised an important issue. It didn't happen again."

You may already have an organization in which people are comfortable raising difficult issues. If not, you can create that environment simply by creating such a policy. Even if you think most people are comfortable coming forward, it never hurts to explicitly articulate the policy.

Call on Everyone

In one TV newsroom where I worked, the boss held a meeting every morning at eight thirty. Reporters and producers crowded into his modest office, shoulder to shoulder, and he would go around the room, calling on each person for an "idea for the day." Knowing you would always be called upon was highly motivating. You didn't come without an idea. The boss jotted those ideas on a legal pad and then doled out the day's news assignments. Naturally, those who contributed good ideas got to cover those stories. This made for better meetings and a better newsroom.

Even people who are happy to participate in meetings may not always come to the table with something unless they're *asked*. There is a difference between participating and showing up with a new idea or insight. The leader can spark creativity just by putting people on notice that they must come prepared to do more than discuss what other people offer.

Throw Your Cares Away

People frequently come to meetings with so much on their plates that they cannot fully participate. They're too concerned about what was happening before the meeting or what's happening afterward. One executive came up with a solution to that distraction. At the beginning of a meeting, he asks people to jot down the top two or three business problems that are on their minds—and then throw them away! They literally pass a trash basket around the room so that people can toss their crumpled notes into the basket.

An alternative is to pass the notes around and have others write down quick solutions. This meeting leader will go so far as to throw candy at participants who seem to be "losing it" during the meeting to wake them up. Creative approaches can send a great message and help people focus on the issue of the moment. A fun approach to throwing cares away may be the reminder people need to stay in the moment.

Summary

■ **Last-minute tip:** Create a practical agenda that includes the purpose of the meeting, a list of participants, brief descriptions of discussion items, and time allotments. Keep your own time line next to each item during the meeting to assure that you stay on track.

■ **If you have more time:** Check in with influential people prior to the meeting to uncover concerns, deal with objections, and build consensus.

■ **Plan for ongoing improvement:** Read books on meeting management, and recommend them to your leadership team. Hold workshops on meeting management, or make the skill part of the individual coaching plans of leaders in the organization. Consider establishing a written meeting policy for the organization.

14

Conversations

"All CEOs should have a camera follow them around for a week. Most would be amazed at how they really come across."
—CHRIS MOORE, CEO of Live Planet

CHRIS MOORE, A TELEVISION and film producer with credits including *Good Will Hunting*, launched Live Planet as a start-up venture with Ben Affleck, Matt Damon, and Sean Bailey. Moore was new in the CEO role at the time Live Planet's reality television series "Project Greenlight" was filmed, a show in which aspiring screenwriters and movie directors compete. The winners make their movies while the cameras are rolling on them. Moore appeared on "Project Greenlight" as the intense, volatile producer trying to keep people in line. "I was the guy who screamed, yelled, and got angry," he said.

Moore never saw clips during production. It was only when the show aired on the Bravo channel that he saw how ineffective his style was. "I was sitting there seeing how people would just write me off," he said. "I thought I was saying important stuff, but they never did what I suggested. Later I called them up and asked, 'Was it a bad idea?' Most of them said they didn't even remember what I had said. They only remembered that I was ripping their head off."

He recognized that a change was in order. Moore described his new way of interacting with others: "I listen now. I think if you ask around, people are calmer and more relaxed around me." While Moore's behavior was extreme, it's interesting to imagine what would happen to any of us if a camera followed us around for just a week. Even if you never lose your composure, or even raise your voice, what would you learn that you didn't know?

"What CEOs might not realize is that people are editing themselves," Moore stated. "CEOs think they are really listening. But the fact is that once you become CEO, people don't question you or challenge you. It's not that CEOs are ignoring people; nobody is questioning them, or having real conversations."

Conversation Challenges

One of the dangers of being CEO is that your conversations change. The day you become boss, people start choosing their words, or choosing to say nothing at all. They are always glad to invite you into the circle, or to join yours, but often it feels artificial. They wait for your cue, laugh at your jokes, ask you questions, and otherwise try to ingratiate themselves. You know this to be true, because once upon a time, you were not the boss.

Conversation indeed changes when you become the boss. You may already have good conversation skills, but you really need to work hard to have genuine conversations with others once you are CEO, especially with the people who work for you. I have never met a CEO who did not have some effective conversation skills. You can't rise to the top without being able to talk with people. But many executives could do much better. They could ask better questions and really listen a lot more to what others are saying.

Conversation should always be engaging and stimulating—a chance for people to probe, debate, brainstorm, ventilate, deliberate, and consider. Conversation is not just talking; it's a two-way street. Great conversation is an art.

Making Time

"Let us make a special effort to stop communicating with each other so we can have some conversation."

—JUDITH MARTIN, Miss Manners

Modern business life makes it difficult for people to find time to talk to each other. We are so pressured to perform that we don't take the extra minute to have a genuine exchange. I learned a valuable lesson about taking time to have a conversation when I met the CEO of a large, successful financial services firm.

I had worked in his company for three years but had never met him. Someone in his organization scheduled us to meet for a media training session. However, when I arrived, he said that he didn't have three hours to work with me and that he would prefer to sit and talk for an hour. He showed me to a comfortable chair in his office, where we had a wide-ranging conversation on his business; he also shared a lot about his personal life. He'd had an interesting childhood and career. As I shook his hand at the door, I was glad I'd had the chance to get to know him. I believe that I was his last appointment of the day. That evening, he died of a heart attack, at age fifty-three.

Since then, I have tried to stop more often and spend more time with people, even if it's only a minute. While it's challenging to make time, what is the point of having a successful professional life if we just run from phone call to meeting to engagement? Conversations don't have to be lengthy to be worthwhile or appreciated by others. Once you start making time, you realize you can do your work and still get to know people.

A CEO should be comfortable talking to anyone. Peter Rollins, who runs the Chief Executive Club of Boston College, has met dozens of the top CEOs of major public corporations. "Most of them become CEO because of their people skills. They are all very intelligent, hardworking, and pragmatic, but I think they reach the top because they really know how to talk to people and treat them with respect," says Rollins. "The ones you admire are genuinely nice, and interested in other people. They're the kind of people you wouldn't mind sitting down with for a beer."

Genuine Curiosity

> *"You can make more friends in two months by becoming interested in other people than you can in two years by trying to get other people interested in you."*

—DALE CARNEGIE, Author, *How to Win Friends and Influence People*

One common denominator of good conversation is genuine curiosity. Genuine curiosity is more than "active listening." It is a sincere interest in people and their ideas. A person who is genuinely curious truly wants to know more about you and your thoughts. A genuinely curious person asks great questions, listens, and responds. Such people aren't necessarily introverted or extroverted—they are simply, truly curious.

I don't believe you can fake authentic listening. People usually know when your mind is wandering, even if you are looking them in the eye. The "tricks" of active listening—such as nodding and repeating phrases—are often apparent to the speaker. Good conversation is about really listening and getting below the surface where so many people spend most of their time.

When you are CEO, people will naturally steer the conversation to you and your interests, but you must work to turn that equation around. To be a genuine exchange of ideas, conversation must be a two-way street. Vicki Donlan, the publisher of *Women's Business Journal* and founder of two women's business organizations, says, "Business conversation is not about you. It's about the person you're speaking with."

Even if you think you know *about* a person, you do not *know* people until you ask them about themselves. Time and time again, I have been surprised at the answers I receive to simple questions such as, "What was it like to grow up in your hometown?" or "Why did you move to that city?" I've learned that my assumptions about a person are often wrong. Assumptions are conversation killers. They keep us from tapping into the genuine curiosity that leads to good conversations.

Genuine curiosity creates a powerful dynamic. People know when you're truly interested in them. And when you are, you don't ever have to put on an act. You don't have to remind yourself to make eye contact or smile: it comes naturally.

Starting a Conversation

It isn't enough to know how to *have* a conversation; you have to know how to *start* one. *Where* you start a conversation—your opening question—is not so important. What's important is to *start*. You need to take the plunge. No one likes to go first, so most people stand around waiting for others to do it. When you take the initiative, people are grateful.

A private wealth-management firm always invited the wife of one of the company's executives to events. Everyone knew that she would be the first to say hello, to offer a hand, or to help someone find a seat. "She always acted as if she were greeting people in her own home," said the event manager. "She was better than most of our salespeople." Be *first*. Take the initiative. People appreciate it when you make the effort.

What questions can you ask, or what topics can you offer? You don't have to talk about the weather, unless there's a hurricane in the area. Ask what brings the person to the event, or what the person's connection is to the other people there. Ask whether the person has ever been to this restaurant, city, or place before or heard this speaker or music group before. Ask people where they are from or where they live. The first question carries less weight than the second and third.

Following Up with Other Great Questions

Once the conversation is under way, you want to ask questions that get to a deeper level. The purpose of many networking situations is to help you find common ground. The reason most people don't enjoy social conversation is that it never gets below the surface. Most conversations are dull because people don't know how to ask pertinent questions.

Good questions demonstrate your genuine interest in other people. You stand out when you ask probing, thought-provoking questions, because so few people do. Good questions are also critical to leadership, because you find out what's really going on and learn things you would never know otherwise.

A good question often begins with the word *how* or *why*. Those words help you probe more deeply into an issue or topic. They help you better understand people and situations. You want to understand more about people's values and beliefs, their reasons for taking actions, and the consequences of those actions, as well as their hopes, plans, and dreams. I will sometimes ask a person, "Why did you decide to . . . " or "How did you feel when . . . ," just to take it to a deeper level. I have found that most people are delighted to go deeper. You should not be afraid to ask. Most people are longing for a conversation that is really about something, especially if it's about them.

Active Listening

"If you wish to win a man over to your ideas, first make him your friend."

—Abraham Lincoln, 16th U.S. President

Active listening is not just about stopping and allowing the other person to speak. Active listening is turning up your sensitivity to substance and tone so that you absorb the *meaning* of what a person has said. It's the little things you hear—the unusual, remarkable, or unexpected. When you hear it, pick up on it and pursue it with another question or observation. The only way to truly listen is to turn up your sensitivity to substance and tone. Read between the lines, and try to fully understand.

Active listening also means giving people time to fully express themselves without interruption. Don't just allow them to finish; leave a little space, a pause, before you dive in. Also at the end of a conversation, provide an opportunity for the person to say something else before you say good-bye. My television agent, Ken Fishkin, is a master at this. At the end of every telephone call or conversation, he asks, "Is there anything else we need to talk about?"

Active listening in a social situation means never having to put on an act. You don't ever have to fake your interest in others if you are really listening. You don't have to pretend, because you really are there with them. You don't have to remind yourself to make eye contact or smile. It will just happen. You do not fool people if you do other things while you're supposed to be listening. If you read your e-mail or do other work while talking on the phone, the other person will know. Moreover, multi-tasking when you're supposed to be listening usually prolongs the conversation, so it isn't even efficient. You don't save time; you waste it when you try to listen and do other things.

Finding Common Ground

> *"The nice thing about being a celebrity is that if you bore people, they think it's their fault."*
>
> —HENRY KISSINGER, Former Secretary of State

In every conversation, you are looking for a common thread that will lead to a two-way exchange. It's a lot more fun when you find a topic of mutual interest—something you can discuss in depth. Once you do, you have the opportunity for an interesting talk. That means you have a chance to really get to know the person.

Finding common ground is easier with people who are like you. But as CEO, you need to make the effort to find it with everyone. With employees, for example, reaching common ground helps build trust. Avoid falling into one-way conversations in which people ask your opinion and you oblige.

Moving on to Business

Many clients ask how to successfully move from social topics to business topics. There are plenty of ways to do this, even if you are meeting someone for the first time. Some of my favorite general questions about business are simple:

- "Tell me about your business."
- "How long have you been with your current firm?"
- "What did you do prior to that?"
- "Who are your customers/clients?"
- "How do you typically find new business?"
- "What are some of the challenges facing your industry now?"

Most people like to talk about their business. So, you need only ask.

Be Informed

Conversation is easy when you are up on current events, politics, sports, entertainment, travel, and other subjects that people enjoy discussing. People gravitate to circles where groups are talking about something interesting. You don't have to work the room when you have something to talk about; the conversation comes to *you*.

The simple advice here is to make time to read books, watch movies, pursue hobbies, try new restaurants, and travel. Have fun. Be interested. Plug in. It not only makes you a better conversationalist but also makes you a happier person.

Ask Advice

Some of the most rewarding conversations happen when you ask a person for advice. People are flattered by the request. You can often find an opening in any conversation to ask what the person would recommend or suggest. If you learn that someone just built an addition to his or her home, ask for suggestions on working with a contractor. If you have just heard about the person's vacation, ask what you should see or where you should eat if you go.

Seeking advice gives you a good reason to initiate a call, whether you know the person or not. If you have even a remote connection, many people will give you a few minutes of their time, if you ask. You should be specific about what you need, take only a few minutes, and send a thank-you note after the call. It is worth asking because you never know what will happen. I have developed wonderful business relationships with people that began with a phone call for advice.

Make a Graceful Exit

To paraphrase singer Paul Simon, there must be fifty ways to leave a conversation. You should never feel guilty about saying good-bye, especially at a networking event, conference, or party. People are there to mix and mingle. After a good conversation, you should shake hands, say adios, and move on.

There is no established time limit for social conversation, but typically the range is five to ten minutes. That gives the parties enough time to get to know each other without dominating each other's time. If you want to carry on, that's great: it gives you an opportunity to follow up later by saying, "I would love to talk with you about this further. Could I call your office, or take you out for coffee?"

A Few Rules
- Keep the good-bye short and simple.
- Make the other person feel great.
- If you want to follow up, say so.
- If you don't want to follow up, just end it there with best wishes and good-bye.
- Don't make the excuse to go to the restroom, bar, or anywhere else the person can follow.
- Always shake hands at good-bye to make it feel like a proper ending.

Here are a few examples of the fifty ways to leave a conversation:

- "It has been great meeting you. I really enjoyed our conversation."
- "It's been a pleasure. I'll see you at the next meeting."

- "Thank you for that information. Could you send me the phone number?"
- "You have a great business idea. If you'll give me your card, I'll keep you in mind."

Conversation Tips

This concluding section highlights some other wisdom I have gleaned from CEOs about conversation.

Play Golf

Tom Goemaat had just taken over as president and CEO of Shawmut Design and Construction, when one of the company's biggest customers called to set up a golf game. The same customer called several more times to schedule breakfasts, golf outings, and dinners. Since the two were not close friends, Tom was curious about why the customer wanted to spend so much time together.

Finally, the customer asked, "Do you know why we do this stuff?"

"Not really," Tom replied.

"We do it because we need to have a relationship built on more than just projects. When we run into a problem—and we will—we have a real relationship, so we can solve the problem," the customer said.

"It explained so much," Tom told me. "And it changed the way I approached these outings. As CEO, you don't play golf to try to close a deal. You don't play golf to hash things out. You just play golf. You talk a little. You get to know people."

Break Bread

Larry Lucchino, CEO of the Boston Red Sox, holds roundtables for six or eight baseball players once a month, where they break bread with the team's manager and the rest of the owners. "Having food and drink is a good idea," he said. "People need to see each other regularly. You have to develop a feel for each other."

Julia Child, the legendary cookbook author who brought French cooking to American television in the 1960s and '70s, almost always entertained guests in her kitchen. She didn't bother to set the table in the dining room, because she knew if her guests were out there while she was cooking, she would miss out on the conversation. Breaking bread together, whether it's at a fancy restaurant or your kitchen table, is one of the best conversation stimulants. Never underestimate the power of food to create the atmosphere for lively conversation.

Think While You're Shaving

Tom O'Neill, president and CEO of O'Neill Associates, tries to have breakfast every morning with someone he has never met or hasn't seen in a long time. As he is getting dressed and shaving, he says, "I think about what might be important to this person. I prepare mentally in the morning for the things that I might say. If you're going to get respect, you have to give respect, and the best way you can do that is to prepare for each conversation."

Taking the time to think about a conversation, and to consider what you would like to learn or accomplish, pays off. Part of preparing for your day is preparing for the conversations you know you will have. You flatter people if you come to the conversation having thought about them. People like to know you have their interests in mind before you walk through the door.

Talking to Celebrities

As a CEO, you will have a chance to meet well-known people. The best approach to these conversations is to be the same person you always are and to discuss topics anyone would want to discuss. I learned when I was a reporter that most actors, authors, athletes, and politicians don't want to talk about themselves all the time. People often barrage them with questions about their celebrity status; they get tired of it, and it makes them uncomfortable.

Dennis Lehane, a New England–born author, saw his star status elevate when his book *Mystic River* became an Oscar-winning film. Not long after, I watched people at a fund-raising event fall all over him. They cornered him so he never moved from one spot all night. Imagine how any of us would react to that. Celebrities are just people. You can ask about their careers and opinions, but find a way to broaden your conversation.

Summary

- **Last-minute tip:** Take the next conversation one level deeper, by using a *how* or *why* question to find out more.

- **If you have more time:** Look at your appointment calendar, make note of the people with whom you will meet tomorrow, and think about the conversations in advance; do some research or take something along to let them know you were thinking about them.

- **Plan for ongoing improvement:** Make a point to take one extra minute near the end of your conversations to ask how the other person is doing or if there is "anything else we need to talk about before we say good-bye."

PART 3

The Strategies

Become a Great Speaker by

Making a Plan and Working It

"Don't stay in bed, unless you can make money in bed."

—GEORGE BURNS, Actor and Comedian

15

Ten Things You Can Do to Guarantee Success

"The way to develop self-confidence is to do the thing you fear
and get a record of successful experiences behind you.
Destiny is not a matter of chance, it is a matter of choice;
it is not a thing to be waited for, it is a thing to be achieved."

—WILLIAM JENNINGS BRYAN, American Lawyer and Speaker

THIS CHAPTER DESCRIBES TEN helpful actions and behaviors that will bring you closer to your speaking goals. Use these recommendations as a guide to stay on target, keep your goals in view, and get to the next level with your speaking plan.

Tip 1: You Chose This Book for a Reason — Honor It

I do not believe that you are reading this book by accident; whether you received it as a gift, picked it up at the airport kiosk, or bought it online, it found you. It found you for good reason. There is a powerful force at work in your life that will allow you to develop your leadership potential.

Pay attention to that force, and honor it. Whether the book was a present or a purchase, it is an investment in your success. If you want to grow that investment, do something more: research and write a speech that truly reflects your beliefs and values; start a story journal; take an acting class to build confidence; hire a speaking coach, media trainer, speechwriter, or wardrobe consultant—anyone who can help you succeed. Whether you are a CEO now or want to be one someday, commit to doing what it takes. That will move you from *wishing* to *becoming*.

Tip 2: Delegate, Delete, or Delay

To make time for this investment, you must put the related actions on your to-do list and put the corresponding appointments on your calendar. You have to make speaking a priority, and you may have to place it higher than other activities currently on your program. You absolutely must create a to-do list and schedule appointments. You know how this works: if you say to a friend, "We'll have to get together for lunch," it doesn't happen; if you both choose a date, and put it in writing, it does. The calendar creates commitment.

Where do you find the time? How do you elbow some more activities into an already busy schedule? My answer to that is: delegate, delete, or delay. This is an approach that allows you to reset priorities and feel confident that the items that have moved down your list will get done one way or another. It's a matter of deciding what you can give to someone else, get rid of, or put off for a while.

While writing this book, I used "delegate, delete, or delay" on a few projects at home. For example, although I wanted to plant a perennial garden in the backyard, I didn't have time over the summer. I *deleted* going to the garden center because I knew I would be tempted to buy perennials that I didn't have time to plant. Then, when the weeds in that part of the yard grew to Jack-and-the-Beanstalk proportions, I asked my daughter to help out. Weeding was *delegated*. We considered hiring a landscape designer to help us create a better environment, but finding and meeting with the designer would take time. We *delayed* the project and lived with less than perfection. Some weeds look like flowers anyway.

I have sat with many clients and looked over their calendars to apply this strategy. These executives are frequently amazed at how delegating, deleting, or delaying projects and activities that are not mission-critical frees up oodles of time. We all have stuff we can dispose of in these ways. You don't need a coach to do this. Look through your calendar. Choose some items that are not essential or that someone else can do. Once you start applying this system, you will find it is so liberating that you will want to do it regularly.

Tip 3: Assemble Your Team

There is nothing like a team of people on your side to help you achieve your goals. You do not have to learn to speak like a CEO all by yourself. You are responsible for making it happen, but you don't have to do it alone. Among the people who could assist you are the following pros:

- Speaker coach
- Media trainer
- Speechwriter
- Mentor
- Wardrobe consultant
- Comedy writer
- PR person
- Fitness trainer
- Voice coach

Bring in high-caliber professionals to support you in your growth and to give you perspective in the areas you are developing. The encouragement you get from them will keep you moving steadily toward your destination. You will get there twice as fast if you have the right people working with you.

Tip 4: Treat Your Personal Coaching Program like a Fitness Program

One CEO I interviewed said speaker coaching is a lot like going to the gym: "You may not enjoy it going in, but you will feel exhilarated coming out." That's an appropriate analogy. The feeling of accomplishment in learning to speak well is powerful.

If you treat your personal coaching program like a fitness program, you will succeed. Trainers advise clients to pick a goal, make a plan, tell a friend, and track their progress. You can do the same with this program. Every ounce of effort you put in will pay off. Once you start, keep going. As Thomas Edison said, "Genius is 1 percent inspiration and 99 percent perspiration."

Tip 5: While You're at It, Get into Top *Physical* Condition, Too

Being in great physical condition makes you feel relaxed and more confident. Staying in shape gives you the energy to meet the demands of your job, including public speaking. You sleep better and feel mentally sharp. You appear confident, because you like the way you look. Your clothes fit, and you tend to buy beautiful clothing that suits you and enhances your image as a leader. Fitness sends a strong message about your self-image; it says you respect yourself, are organized and disciplined, and have the energy it takes to do the work. No matter how busy you are, make time to work out.

When you start a fitness program, you are always advised to begin slowly so you don't injure yourself. Injuries are one of the main reasons people fall short of their fitness goals. If you start slowly, you can avoid a major setback. You can get a great workout in so many ways: going to the health club, playing sports, walking, hiking, or swimming. During the week, park you car at the far end of the lot; take the stairs instead of the elevator. On the weekend, get outside and do something physical. It's your overall approach to fitness, not the thirty minutes you commit to a routine, that will keep you in top shape.

If you have a regular exercise regime, that's great. Keep it up. If you don't, I suggest you apply the system discussed earlier: delegate, delete, or delay. Make time to make fitness a priority; make the commitment to your physical health and well-being. Staying fit sets a powerful example for the people who work with you, too. Fitness is good for business.

Tip 6: Push Yourself with Stretch Goals in Your Coaching Program

As you gain confidence, you will want to set some stretch goals. After you master one skill, try something new. Don't be afraid to fail. Sometimes it feels easier to play it safe and follow the formula rather than risk looking foolish. But that won't build your confidence or help you enjoy speaking publicly.

Stretching helps you find out what you're capable of doing. Perfection is not the goal—effectiveness is. Don't worry about failing. As novelist Anna Quindlen says, "The thing that is really hard—and really amazing—is giving up on being perfect and beginning the work of becoming yourself."

If you feel stale, shake it up. Try stepping out from behind the podium and speaking without notes. Use a prop. Tell a funny story about yourself. Be candid and say what everybody else is thinking. Accept a speaking engagement at a major conference. Say yes to an interview with a major daily newspaper. There are countless ways to shake things up. Doing so will stretch your mental muscles.

Tip 7: Don't Stop

Winston Churchill once said, "If you are going through hell, keep going." Sometimes you will be disappointed by a speech or presentation. You might be misquoted in the newspaper. You may wish you had said something different in a meeting. Let it go. Learn from mistakes. Nobody is perfect. You cannot anticipate every hazard.

Dust yourself off and get back out there. Those missteps can provide prime material for your next event! I have made lemonade out of lemons by taking my mistakes and turning them into stories for speeches. If you're not failing, you're not trying. Don't stop, even if it seems hard. Someday, when someone comes up to you and says, "You make speaking look so easy," you'll just look at the person and smile.

Tip 8: Believe You Can

Architect Frank Lloyd Wright once said, "The thing always happens that you really believe in; and the belief in a thing makes it happen." We rarely accomplish much before we *believe* that it can be done. We have few guarantees in life, but we know that if we do not start a journey, we will not reach a destination.

Whatever your goal is in this program, you must believe that achieving it is possible. Sometimes you have to take a leap of faith, but on the other side of the leap is *action*. True belief gets you out of bed. True belief makes you roll up your sleeves and do it. Tap into belief and you will find motivation.

Tip 9: Enjoy

> "*The secret of joy in work is contained in one word*—excellence. *To know how to do something well is to enjoy it.*"
>
> —Pearl Buck, American Writer

I asked one CEO who speaks well what he thought other CEOs should know about speaking. "You have to enjoy doing it," he observed. "It comes across to an audience."

I know what you're thinking: speaking well is one thing; *enjoying* it is another. If you hate public speaking, or can't imagine taking pleasure in talking to reporters, think again—it *can* be fun. The secret is to do it *well*. Doing anything well is its own reward. Plus, you get positive feedback. You may never love speaking or presenting, but you will feel the joy of getting *results*.

Tip 10: Take Time to Celebrate Success

Successful talk-show host and actress Oprah Winfrey says, "The more you praise and celebrate your life, the more there is in life to celebrate." When you work hard on anything, you should stop to celebrate. You should enjoy the fruits of your labor.

I always encourage clients to reward themselves after they have worked hard on a major project. Find some small but significant way to celebrate an achievement. If you have worked hard at writing and practicing a speech that is subsequently well received, take an afternoon off. If you make a presentation and win business, go shopping or out to dinner. Rewarding yourself tells your brain, "This is fun!" and motivates you to forge ahead and do more.

Your coaching program is not a marathon with a big reward at the *end*. It's a journey with milestones that you should mark. Celebrate each success as you become the speaker and leader you want to be. Garner the encouragement from your support team, commit to your goals, and tackle your obstacles. Let the model coaching programs in Chapter 16 serve as guides when you're creating your personalized speaking plan. Invest in yourself and you *will* become a better speaker.

16

Five Coaching Plans

"If I had eight hours to chop down a tree,
I would spend six hours sharpening my axe."

—ABRAHAM LINCOLN, 16th U.S. President

IN THIS FINAL CHAPTER, you will find five sample coaching plans. These should serve as blueprints for creating your own. The sample plans have various goals and time lines. I offer them not as plans you should execute, but as models for customizing your own program for learning how to speak like a CEO.

Think about what you want to achieve. Write it down. What will it take to get there? The more specific your plan, the more likely you are to be successful in the execution. Integrate these activities into your to-do list or calendar. Check them off, week by week, month by month. Soon you will look back and say, "Hey, I actually *did* that."

You may want to work with a coach. A coach can help you every step of the way: assess your needs, design a plan, guide your learning, give you feedback, and celebrate your success.

If you don't use a speaker coach, a media trainer, or another outside professionals, bring together an internal team. No matter where you are in your career, other people can help. Look at Tiger Woods. He had help constructing the best game in golf—from coach Butch Harmon. When he broke off his relationship with Harmon, his game suffered. Sports commentators often suggested that he bring back Butch. All of us, at every stage, can benefit from having other people to help keep us on top of our game.

Three-Month Plan: Keynote Speaking

Project: Deliver an outstanding keynote speech to a major business group

Goals
- Write and speak with clarity
- Learn to use stories to make points
- Develop humor and be comfortable with it
- Make better eye contact
- Appear completely comfortable and relaxed in front of the audience
- Use voice more effectively
- Speak more conversationally

Time allotted: Ten hours per month, 30 hours total

First-month activities: Initial consultation with coach. Videotape/skills-gap analysis; discuss audience and theme of speech with writer; write stories, anecdotes, and elements; research and write first draft, review; start personal binder for speaker stories.

Second-month activities: Videotape next draft, review; work on voice, body language, and gestures; practice telling stories, add humor, read book on voice, listen to tape of good speakers.

Third-month activities: Practice at a podium, videotape/review with coach, practice at home; internalize messages, complete final draft, conduct dress rehearsal, review outcomes with coach.

Six-Month Plan: Presentation Skills

Project: Deliver a technical/business presentation on a new initiative to investors, employees, or customers

Goals
- Develop confident, relaxed presentation style
- Present technical material so that everyone understands
- Show relevance of solutions to audience's needs
- Learn techniques for persuading an audience
- Stand in front without a podium, with confidence
- Use hands and gestures effectively
- Improve professional appearance

Time allotted: Eight hours per month, 48 hours total

First-month activities: Meet with coach for skills-gap analysis. Research audience and topic, convene strategic planning meeting, outline presentation, read book on professional image, meet with wardrobe consultant.

Second-month activities: Second strategic planning session, sit in on conference presentations to watch good speakers, pick up new techniques.

Third-month activities: Create talking points. Third strategic planning meeting, talk through presentation, practice at home, read a book on PowerPoint presentations.

Fourth-month activities: Videotape a dress rehearsal of the presentation, get feedback from team and coach, practice in front of mirror, practice voice with tape recorder at home.

Fifth-month activities: Dress rehearsal, feedback and revisions, feedback on content and style of presentation from coach.

Six-month activities: Review video of presentation with coach, assess progress, and set goals for next six months.

Six-Month Plan: Media Training

Project: Media tour to publicize a major new product/service/innovation

Goals
- Develop confidence speaking to reporters
- Present ideas clearly and concisely

- Manage interviews with confidence
- Develop new strategies to prepare for interviews
- Speak in sound bites with energy and enthusiasm
- Deliver opinion effectively
- Know how to handle tough questions
- Show more on-camera poise for television
- Stay on message and deliver key points without wandering

Time allotted: Four hours per month, twenty-four hours total

First-month activities: Meet with PR/Communications staff to discuss strategic focus, message; meet with coach to develop talking points; review talking points and practice out loud; read a book on how to manage the media.

Second-month activities: Meet with coach/PR team to write up anticipated questions; videotape a practice session, a "mock interview"; refine talking points.

Third-month activities: Practice delivering talking points into a tape recorder, listen to voice; practice with coach, second mock interview, review body language, voice; read a book on camera technique, videoconferencing, and television.

Fourth-month activities: Dress rehearsal: news conference, videotape and review with coach and PR; dress rehearsal: one-on-one interviews, videotape and review with coach.

Fifth-month activities: News conference, videotape; interviews, videotape; review with coach and get feedback, assess progress.

Sixth-month activities: Review newspaper, magazine clippings with PR/Communications staff; meet with coach to assess progress and set goals for next six months.

Six-Month Plan: Presentations, Speech, Media

Projects: Give outstanding presentations to the board; improve relationships with unhappy customers who had a bad experience; build support in business community through media interviews; motivate and inspire employees after period of bad news

Goals

- Speak with clarity about vision
- Appear comfortable and confident with board of directors
- Fine-tune answers to tough questions from unhappy customers
- Deliver strong messages to media
- Speak conversationally to employees
- Motivate and inspire people to overcome a difficult situation

Time allotted: Eight hours per month, 48 hours total

First-month activities: Write detailed communication goals for the year; personal history interview with coach; videotape board presentation and receive skills-gap analysis; read a book on public speaking skills.

Second-month activities: Discuss talking points for media with PR/Communications; review talking points with coach; prepare or review Power-Point slides; practice at home.

Third-month activities: Dress rehearsal: board presentation, videotape; practice and review with coach; read book on media skills; set up customer meetings.

Fourth-month activities: Videotape mock media interview; compile list of tough questions from customers, discuss strategies, refine talking points with coach.

Fifth-month activities: Review clippings and/or video of real media interviews, role-play to prepare for customer meetings, record it on audiocassette and play back, refine talking points, read book on negotiations.

Six-month activities: Conduct meetings with customers, review outcomes with coach, start preparing talking points for next board meeting, practice at home.

Twelve-Month Plan: Leadership Communication Skills

Goal: Prepare to move up to a new, larger role in the company by improving all aspects of communication: speeches, presentations, media interviews, leading meetings, conversation skills

Time allotted: Eight hours per month, ninety-six hours total

First-month activities: Personal history interview, coach conducts 360-degree interviews with colleagues, direct reports, supervisors, and top management; start writing professional goals.

Second-month activities: Coach presents findings of 360-degree interviews, review findings; discuss goals and strategies; work on to-do list based on goals and strategies.

Third-month activities: Deliver a presentation and videotape it; assess skill gaps; get constructive feedback.

Fourth-month activities: Review videotape; assess content and style of presentation; practice new skills; prepare speech with talking points and stories; research facts and anecdotes.

Fifth-month activities: Videotape draft of speech; work on content and style issues; revise speech and practice again; deliver speech.

Sixth-month activities: Review videotape of speech for content and style; get additional tips and recommendations; create agenda for meeting by determining issues, areas of conflict, and stakeholders.

Seventh-month activities: Go through agenda; practice talking points; role-play discussions; discuss premeeting stakeholders to contact to lay groundwork; discuss techniques for managing difficult issues. Write introduction and important talking points.

Eighth-month activities: Review outcome of meeting and strategies that succeeded; determine business event of importance and discuss participants, conversations, and background. Review business etiquette; determine conversation topics; role-play conversations and videotape them.

Ninth-month activities: Prepare talking points and questions for media interview; practice answers; review interview techniques; give media interviews.

Tenth-month activities: Review videotape and clippings of media interview; identify what worked and didn't. Research, write, review, and practice the major speech.

Eleventh-month activities: Practice delivery of major speech, videotape, review with coach.

Twelfth-month activities: Review goals and assess progress, make plans for next year.

Make the Journey Your Own

"A journey of a thousand miles must begin with a single step."

—LAO-TZU, Founder of Taoism

As you look over these plans, you will see that they vary in length: three months, six months, and one year. Your program is your own. Modify the goals, time lines, and activities to meet your needs. By using the techniques in the previous chapters—such as delegate, delete, or delay—you can create and customize a plan that will set you on the right path to accomplishing your speaking goals.

Taking the first step on your path requires two beliefs: (1) that you're capable of achieving your goals, and (2) that your efforts will make a difference in advancing your career. You *are* capable, and your efforts *will* make a tremendous difference. While the end result for which you're striving may seem daunting, just keep in mind that the strategies you've learned in this book will help break down the process into tasks you can work on day to day.

Remember, there is no such thing as a natural-born speaker. You hold the power to become the successful leader you want to be when you have the tools and skills to communicate effectively with all of your audiences. It's up to you to decide what kind of speaker and leader you will be. Don't be afraid to take that first stride and make the journey your own.

Appendix A

Checklists

CHECKLISTS CAN HELP you prepare your speech, presentation, or media interview. In addition, you can use checklists to assist you in evaluating your skills as they develop. The checklists in this section are divided into two categories: content and style. As you review a tape of your speech, presentation, or interview, use these as a guideline. You can also ask a coach, colleague, or friend to refer to these checklists as an aid in assessing your performance.

Speech/Presentation Checklist

Content

___ Story or anecdote to open
___ Clear statement of theme or agenda
___ Well-organized and to-the-point
___ Focus on the audience
___ Clear statement of audience benefits
___ Inclusive language
___ Good use of stories and anecdotes
___ Interesting facts and illustrations
___ Word pictures and descriptive language

___ Current events or news
___ Useful handouts to support presentation
___ Eye-catching, easy-to-see visuals
___ Useful, relevant information

Style
___ Conversational
___ Energy
___ Relaxed posture
___ Open body language
___ Effective gestures
___ Smile
___ Eye contact
___ Purposeful movement
___ Interesting voice, inflection
___ Pleasant tone and volume
___ Appropriate pace, pauses, and phrasing
___ No vocal habits like *um*

Media Interview Checklist

Use this checklist when preparing for a media interview to remind you what you can include. As you practice the interview, you can ask a coach or trusted colleague to check items and write comments.

You can also use this checklist to assess your performance if you have a video of your news conference or interview. Check off the elements that you notice and write comments on the right about how effective they are.

Content
___ Compelling facts
___ Relevant, interesting, timely
___ Brief and to the point
___ Information of concern to people outside the organization
___ Clear message

_____ Supporting facts

_____ Simple language

_____ Answers to tough questions

_____ Short, concise sound bites

_____ Flags for important ideas

_____ Bridges to main talking points

Style

_____ Conversational

_____ Energetic delivery

_____ Good posture

_____ Open body language

_____ Pleasant facial expressions

_____ Steady eye contact with the camera (if remote) or reporter (if in-person)

_____ Arms and hands quiet

_____ Interesting voice inflection

_____ Appropriate pace, pauses, and phrasing

_____ Pleasant tone and volume

_____ Comfortable appearance

Appendix B

Frequently Asked Questions

THIS APPENDIX IS A quick reference guide to questions that Bates Communications is frequently asked.

Q: How much should I practice a speech?

A: Professional speakers practice their speeches out loud as many as a dozen times before they deliver them to a live audience. If you want to improve, use that as a guideline.

Q: I admire funny speakers, but I don't think I'm funny. What can I do?

A: Anyone can be funny. You don't have to be a comedian. Use self-effacing humor. Notice painful situations, and turn them around with the techniques described in Chapter 9. Audiences appreciate appropriate humor; it prepares them to listen and sets you apart as a confident speaker.

Q: I don't know any good stories. How can I find some for my speeches?

A: The best place to start is your own experience. That's a powerful technique. Also, take note of stories about people around you that could inspire others or illustrate important values.

Q: Should I write out my speech word for word, or work from note cards?

A: It depends on the speech. An important keynote or eulogy might be written out word for word. An informal presentation to employees can be outlined on note cards.

Q: I like to speak off-the-cuff. Why do I have to practice?

A: Great speakers who look as if they are speaking extemporaneously usually have practiced the main parts of their talk. Practice helps you make your points clearly and helps you avoid being too wordy or meandering.

Q: I speak well to small groups, but I feel nervous with a large crowd. How can I reduce these nerves?

A: The solution is to practice and learn your speech well. We feel anxious when we are unprepared. It will also help you to practice the speech at the podium and visualize the audience.

Q: How can I be more effective in getting my message across to the media?

A: Write down the questions you expect to be asked, even the ones you don't want to answer. Prepare your talking points, and role-play with someone to practice delivering the talking points and handling the tough questions.

Q: How can I avoid getting trapped by a tough question from a reporter?

A: Never say, "No comment," because it makes you sound evasive. Tell the reporter why you cannot answer, or answer honestly. If you try to avoid it, reporters *will* ask again.

Q: Is it OK to speak to reporters off the record to make sure they get it right?

A: Speaking off the record to the media can be tricky, especially if you go on and off the record during the same interview—it can create confusion. If you know the reporter, you can tell him or her clearly that you will provide background, not for attribution. Be sure to have reporters verbally acknowledge their understanding of this before you speak.

Q: How can I avoid being misquoted?
A: Learn to *flag* important messages, speak clearly, and repeat your main messages.

Q: What should I look for in a coach?
A: Check out the person's professional experience, client list, references, books, and articles. Interview candidates to see whether you connect. Chemistry is important. Discuss the prospective coach's methods, and assess the person's ability to provide honest, constructive feedback.

Appendix C

Communication and Leadership

Results of Nationwide Survey: "How Does Your Boss Communicate?" Bates Communications, Inc.

This is a brief summary of the findings of a nationwide online survey of 293 professionals in 2004 regarding communication and leadership in the workplace. The survey included both closed- and open-ended questions. Each respondent was asked to rate his or her boss on ten dimensions of leadership and communication. There were also questions about the leadership of the respondent's organization and about communication styles in the workplace. Finally, respondents were asked open-ended questions—one about what makes an authentic leader and one asking what advice they would give to help the leaders of their organizations become better communicators.

Communication Is Critical

Respondents were virtually unanimous when it came to rating the importance of effective communication. Effective communication is clearly a requirement for effective leadership:

How important is it for the leader of your organization to communicate effectively?

    91.5% Very important—it's a critical dimension of leadership
      7.8% Somewhat important—it contributes to our success
      .7% Not very important—other skills are much more critical

Trust in Leaders Is High, but More Leadership Is Needed

Overall, our sample was split between strong and moderate levels of trust in the leadership of respondents' organizations. Only a few people said they don't really trust their leadership:

Overall, how much do you trust the leadership of your organization?

    44.7% A great deal—they are very trustworthy
    43.7% Moderately—they try, but people are sometimes skeptical
    11.6% I don't trust them—they have done little to inspire trust or win confidence

In particular, the heads of most respondents' organizations are vested with the mantle of true leadership:

How surprised would you be if the head of your company were to speak to the organization, clearly articulating a new direction and inspiring everyone to follow?

    65.5% Not surprised—this person is an authentic voice of leadership
    26.3% Somewhat surprised—we rarely see that ability to articulate or inspire
     8.2% Shocked—this leader just doesn't know how to do that

Beyond the top rank, however, our respondents found their organizations somewhat lacking; less than one-third said they feel their organizations have multiple true voices of leadership:

How would you characterize the voices of leadership in your organization?

    29.0% There are many articulate, inspiring leaders
    49.8% There are some, but we could use more
    21.2% There are few, if any, true voices of leadership here

In sum, top leadership receives good marks, but there is need for more and better voices of leadership *throughout* the ranks of most companies and organizations.

Bosses Need to Improve Communication Skills

Because many professionals deal more closely with their own bosses' style and communication skills than with those of top leadership, we asked our respondents to rate their bosses on a variety of communication dimensions.

Generally speaking, bosses fared a bit lower on specific communication behaviors (listening, speaking skills, leading productive meetings) than on dimensions having to do with personal rapport (humor, candidness) or being the public face of an organization (articulating goals, representing the company). This may indicate that the raw material is there but that specific training in communication skills and techniques can only enhance leaders' ability to lead and persuade.

In this portion of the survey, respondents rated their bosses on ten dimensions, with three evaluative choices:

Please think about your boss or the person to whom you report in your company or organization. Please rate your boss on each dimension, using the following scale:

    Strong   My boss is quite successful at this
    Average My boss tries and sometimes succeeds
    Weak   My boss makes little effort; efforts are largely
                 unsuccessful

Here are the findings, in descending order of "Strong" votes. There were five areas in which the majority gave the boss a "Strong" rating:

Demonstrating a Sense of Humor, When Appropriate
Strong   60.4%
Average   30.7%
Weak   8.9%

Representing the Company at Public Events
Strong   57.3%
Average   30.8%
Weak   11.9%

Being Candid and Straightforward
Strong   54.9%
Average   31.1%
Weak   14.0%

Articulating the Company's Vision and Goals
Strong   54.3%
Average   32.0%
Weak   13.7%

Communicating with Employees on a Human Level
Strong   51.2%
Average   25.9%
Weak   22.9%

Fewer than half gave the boss a strong rating on the remaining five dimensions:

Listening to Comments and Suggestions
Strong   49.8%
Average   32.1%
Weak   18.1%

Giving Good Speeches and Presentations
Strong   48.8%
Average   39.6%
Weak   11.6%

Ability to Motivate and Inspire Others
Strong   43.3%
Average   37.5%
Weak   19.2%

Sharing Critical Information About the Business with Employees
Strong   41.0%
Average   37.9%
Weak   21.1%

Leading and Managing Productive Business Meetings
Strong   40.6%
Average   41.0%
Weak   18.4%

Finally, we asked how respondents figure out what's going on with their bosses. Most said they make these judgments without consulting others, based primarily on words and secondarily on nonverbal cues:

How do you generally tell what's going on with your boss?

52.2%   By listening to what he or she says
32.8%   By observing his or her face, body language, and tone of voice
15.0%   By talking with other people about what they think

Characteristics That Make a Boss a Strong Leader

To better understand what qualities professionals value in a leader, the survey concluded with two open-ended questions. In categorizing the responses, we identified ten key dimensions of leadership. The most frequently mentioned quality by far was honesty/integrity. Because these were open-ended responses, we treat them as qualitative data and don't append numbers, but each of the following dimensions was mentioned by dozens of respondents; integrity (in some guise) was mentioned by well more than half. Here is the leadership value system articulated by our 293 respondents, in roughly descending order:

■ **Integrity.** Responses in this category referred to both business dealings and personal interactions. The words most frequently used by respondents to frame this concept were *honesty, integrity, ethics, fairness, candor, sincerity, trustworthiness,* and *truthfulness*.

■ **Vision.** This dimension comprises having a vision for the organization and being able to articulate it and inspire action, as well as charisma—the ability to inspire and motivate.

■ **Listening.** It's important to be approachable and open to suggestions. Respondents also mentioned traits such as open-mindedness, flexibility, and willingness to listen to everyone's ideas and feedback. They want leaders to seek other points of view and actively listen to what others say (particularly those most intimately involved with a critical issue or type of work).

■ **Giving feedback.** Participants place a priority on giving credit where credit is due, including public praise for a job well done. They cited offering positive feedback when deserved and valuing employees' contributions.

■ **Emotional intelligence.** Treating people well and having empathy and compassion are highly rated. Participants also mentioned being able to relate on a human level to everyone in the organization. Demeanor counts; having a positive attitude and remaining calm under pressure send meaningful signals through the organization. Having obvious passion for the work, a demonstrated commitment to the organization's success, and appreciation for those who contribute to that success are critical.

▪ **Communication skills.** This dimension covers a wide array of talents; in general, the ideal leader is articulate, well spoken, and able to communicate clearly and convincingly with people at all levels of the organization.

▪ **Knowledge and intelligence.** This dimension received fewer mentions, probably due to a presumption that those in a position of organizational leadership have de facto demonstrated intelligence and mastery of their fields. However, quite a few respondents mentioned that an authentic leader needs to be smart in every sense of the word and needs to have extensive knowledge of the substance of his or her field.

▪ **Managerial skills.** Participants mentioned the ability to delegate and allocate resources (monetary, physical, and human resources) for greatest effectiveness and efficiency. They also cited the ability to empower employees and trust them to get the job done—in other words, creating willingness in the organization.

▪ **Follow-through.** Authentic leaders practice what they preach. They walk the walk, and employees watch for this. People want leaders who see projects through to the end; they know when someone spells out goals and just leaves them hanging. Strong leaders are consistently concerned about how things come out, not just how they begin.

▪ **Humility.** No one's perfect, and no one is omniscient. An authentic leader is humble—willing to seek information and advice and to admit mistakes when they occur. An authentic leader is also willing to take appropriate risks; he or she follows through with praise when they pay off and graciously accepts the consequences when they don't, without pointing the finger of blame inappropriately.

Appendix D

The Gettysburg Address: Abraham Lincoln

ONE OF THE GREATEST speeches ever given was also one of the shortest:

Four score and seven years ago our fathers brought forth on this continent, a new nation, conceived in Liberty, and dedicated to the proposition that all men are created equal.

Now we are engaged in a great civil war, testing whether that nation, or any nation so conceived and so dedicated, can long endure. We are met on a great battle-field of that war. We have come to dedicate a portion of that field, as a final resting place for those who here gave their lives that this nation might live. It is altogether fitting and proper that we should do this.

But in a larger sense, we can not dedicate—we can not consecrate—we can not hallow—this ground. The brave men, living and dead, who struggled here, have consecrated it, far above our poor power to add or detract. The world will little note, nor long remember what we say here, but it can never forget what they did here. It is for us the living, rather, to be dedicated here to the unfinished work which they who fought here have thus far so nobly advanced. It is rather for us to be here dedicated to the great task remaining before us—that from these honored dead we take increased devotion to that cause for which they gave the last full measure of devotion—that we here highly resolve that these dead shall not have died in vain—that this nation, under God, shall have a new birth of freedom—and that government of the people, by the people, for the people, shall not perish from the earth.

Index

About the Author

FORMERLY AN AWARD-WINNING television news anchor and reporter, Suzanne Bates is now an executive coach and consultant to business leaders and corporations. Her firm, Bates Communications, Inc., helps clients project an authentic voice of leadership and get a competitive edge in business.

For twenty years, Suzanne was an acclaimed news anchor with major market television stations WBZ-TV Boston, WCAU-TV Philadelphia, and WFLA-TV Tampa-St. Petersburg. She won an AP News Award and was nominated for a Columbia DuPont Award, and over her career, she interviewed thousands of political leaders, CEOs, experts, authors, and celebrities. As a keynote speaker, workshop leader, consultant, and executive coach, she helps clients discover practical, proven techniques to connect with any audience and talk their way to the top.

As President and CEO of Bates Communications, Inc., Suzanne leads a firm that helps businesses communicate with customers, clients, employees, directors, employees, shareholders, and the media. The firm's executive coaching program, workshops, and strategies have been instrumental in helping businesses communicate effectively.

Bates Communications, Inc., has conducted research and written for magazines and newspapers. The firm has published two nationwide surveys, "Credibility, a New Era in Business" in 2002 and "How Does Your Boss Communicate?" in 2004. Suzanne is a frequent commentator on business communication issues. She also occasionally hosts programs on radio stations, including WBUR—Boston's National Public Radio station.

Suzanne is a member of the Leadership Council at Harvard University's Center for Business and Government. She is past president of the Massachusetts Women's Political Caucus, a multipartisan organization devoted to helping women in leadership, and has coached many political leaders in communication skills. She is also a member of the prestigious Boston Club—for senior executive women—and she belongs to the CEO Club of Boston College, as well as the National Speakers Association.

Suzanne has a BS in Radio-TV Journalism from the University of Illinois. She has been an adjunct lecturer on current affairs at Harvard University's Kennedy School of Government and has taught seminars at colleges, including Harvard Business School, Boston University, Boston College, and Babson College.

Suzanne is a dynamic keynote speaker and workshop leader. In addition to her book, *Speak like a CEO: Secrets for Commanding Attention and Getting Results,* she has several CD programs on communication skills, including the six-CD series "Speak like a CEO Toolkit."

Suzanne was born and raised in Danville, Illinois, and now lives in a suburb of Boston, Massachusetts, with her husband and daughter.

Bates Communications, Inc., is located in Wellesley, Massachusetts. You can contact the firm by calling (800) 908-8239 or on the web at www.bates-communications.com. Information about the book, as well as Speak like a CEO retreats, seminars, and executive boot camps, is available at www.speaklikeaceo.com.